USA TODAY
B O O K S

FIRE AT WILL

DeWAYNE WICKHAM

GANNETT CO. INC.
WASHINGTON, D.C. 20044

ISBN 0-944347-20-7

THANKS TO WANDA

BUT for the patience, understanding and love of the woman who is both my wife and best friend, my columns and this book would have suffered greatly. Any credits that are forthcoming as a result of both must be shared with her. The criticisms are mine alone to bear. ■

CONTENTS

CONTENTS

CONTENTS

ABOUT THIS BOOK

first met Jim Geehan in a hotel bar in August 1985, where the two of us had gone to feel each other out. For more than an hour, I stared into his eyes, hoping they might reveal something about the content of his heart.

The vice president of Gannett News Service, Jim said he was in search of a black columnist to bring a different voice to the commentaries his operation produced for Gannett's newspapers. I was there in hopes of landing the job.

The thing I remember most about our conversation is that we never talked specifically about opinion writing. Jim was more interested in me and the things I had to say about the issues and events of the day.

It took him a little more than an hour to take his measure of me.

A week later he called and offered me the job. He wanted me to write a regular column for Gannett News Service. I would be free, he said, to travel across the nation in search of my columns. Free to set my schedule and determine the subjects of my opinion pieces.

So when do I start, I asked him, somewhat disbelieving of his offer.

"Fire at will," he answered dryly.

■

Change, for me, is more frightening than the right hand of Mike Tyson.

Those who are unfortunate enough to connect squarely with the heavyweight champion's vicious fist do not doubt their fate.

But the results of change are a lot less predictable.

So it was that when Nancy Woodhull came to head Gannett News Service, I joined with many of my newsroom colleagues in chafing in her wake.

But like Jim Geehan, Nancy quickly became one of my biggest boosters. With both courage and conviction, she gave me the support I needed to continue my work.

It is probably true that no other black columnist has been given the great leeway Gannett allows me to research and write my columns. Given the professional restraints that many of my black peers are made to suffer, I am doubly grateful for the journalistic freedom Gannett has afforded me — this book being the most recent and notable example.

■

Special thanks to Woodhull, now president of Gannett News Services, and Ron Cohen, executive editor of Gannett News Service, for their support of my columns and this book.

Jerry Langdon, Craig Schwed and Theresa Barry of Gannett News Service and Sid Hurlburt of USA TODAY assisted in preparation of my columns.

The entire staff at Gannett New Media, which published this book, must be thanked, especially Phil Fuhrer, Emilie Davis, J. Ford Huffman, Randy Kirk, Beth Goodrich and Lark Borden.

JoAn Moore, USA TODAY senior format writer, and Tony Bennett, USA TODAY assistant systems editor, provided technical assistance. USA TODAY Managing Editor/Library Dorothy Bland and her staff and Lynn Davis of GNS gave valuable research help. Tom Snoreck of Snoreck Design Group helped with production of the cover.

Also, for their support of this book and continued efforts to make Gannett newsrooms reflect their readers, much appreciation goes to Gannett Chairman, President and Chief Executive Officer John J. Curley; Gannett Executive Vice President/News John C. Quinn; USA TODAY Editor Peter S. Prichard; and USA TODAY Editorial Director John Seigenthaler.

DeWayne Wickham, *August 1989*

PREFACE

was honored when DeWayne Wickham suggested I write the preface for this book. Then, faced with the task of organizing my thoughts, it dawned on me that I was venturing into unknown territory. After all, I make my living standing in front of cameras wearing layers of makeup, trying to appear sincere. Despite this, my friend has asked me to help reveal himself and his work to the readers of this book.

DeWayne and I have spent many hours discussing the plight of our people. We seem to always come to the mutual belief that above all, what we lack most is a forum. All too often black America has allowed someone else to tell our stories, to define our needs, to expose our weaknesses and to reveal our strengths. There is so much said about us by so many others who know so little of what we truly feel.

Since I was a young man, I've been interested in the power of words. No matter how simple or innocent they appear to be, they are immensely potent. What is merely written or spoken goes a long way to establish what is taken to be the truth, and therefore is the primary tool of infinite power. Simply put, he who controls the flow of words to the people, controls the people.

This book is a rare commodity in that it offers social and political commentary from the largely overlooked perspective of a black man. Through its hard-hitting — though sometimes playful — style, it captures the emotional urgency and reality of the times. DeWayne is not a man to shy away from controversy, as you will find. Nor is he reluctant to champion the cause of the oppressed.

From what I have been able to grasp, the best use of the written word does more than present facts. It captures the spirit that drives people to better their lives. Thanks to books like this, the spirit of my people has been aroused.

Tim Reid, *actor-producer*

INTRODUCTION

**VEN** though DeWayne Wickham is only slightly older than me, he is one of my role models. So, I was honored when he asked me to write the introduction to his book.

Ever since we met a few years ago, I have been astounded by his energy and his eye. His energy seems boundless as he balances the tasks of writing a syndicated column, hosting a television talk show and presiding over the National Association of Black Journalists, among his many other activities.

His eye, to paraphrase Hemingway, has a built-in, bull-jive detector, always on the lookout for phonies, racists and con artists. No matter how much you have read about this or that headline-making issue, DeWayne Wickham can give you another thought-provoking angle — and do it with high style.

I read DeWayne's column every chance I get. Few others offer such a grand mixture of the erudition of Frederick Douglass, the courage of Ida B. Wells and the cunning of Spike Lee.

In "Liberating Grenada," for example, he entertains the intriguing thought of Ronald Reagan as prime minister of the embattled island turning his sights to the millions of blacks waiting for similar liberation back here in the United States.

In "Hero of Howard Beach," he retells the tragedy of that neighborhood in Queens by zeroing in on one of its participants, the ring leader of the white teen wolf pack that chased a black man to his death and ruthlessly beat his two companions.

In "A not-so-good Samaritan," unconstrained by ideology of the political right or left, he takes on Mitch Snyder, an icon of the liberal chic, who, in DeWayne's view, "hustles his concern for the poor in much the same way that pimps care for their whores."

Similarly, in "A second-story man," he nails the Rev. Al Sharpton, the Brooklyn minister with the famous James Brown hairdo, as "a crafty manipulator who craves the media spotlight in much the same way that second-story men delight in an open window."

Nor are his media colleagues immune from Wickham's lash. In "Journalistic wilding," he shows how mob frenzy is not limited to violent street hoods. Sometimes the major media do it, too.

But DeWayne Wickham has his soft side, too, tempered with life's often-bitter realities. In "Reluctant hero," he offers a touching tribute to the late Max Robinson, the first black journalist to anchor a television network newscast, and admonishes those of us who, with our unblinking admiration, expected more of him than we would ask of white broadcasters. "We all tended to heap a lot of burdens on Robinson's broad shoulders," writes Wickham.

In the poignant "A story worth telling," he introduces us to a quadriplegic woman who tries to support her children by playing the piano with her tongue, until she runs up against unsympathetic authorities and their anti-begging ordinance. In "A dream deferred," he waxes personal to describe the special pain that comes from seeing one's childhood dreams spoiled by the deadly invasion of drugs into the seemingly pristine world of sports.

When the time comes to make a moral or ethical judgment call, DeWayne asks us to consider alternatives to the easy positions others might offer. In "Misplaced outrage," he dismisses the uproar over depictions of black males in *The Color Purple* as a diversionary dust-up. "I'll save my rage for life's real villains," he says. In "A pregnant cheerleader," he lets his old-fashioned values show in the face of new-wave social policies. "Children in our democratic society have lots of rights," he observes, "but being a pregnant cheerleader should not be one of them."

On the lighter side, DeWayne puts his tongue firmly in his cheek to offer "Do be serious," his own humble advice for Republican presidential candidates who intend to campaign in the black community.

With tongue still in cheek, he introduces us to his alter ego, "Ungawah Jones," an unreconstructed 1960s radical right off the streets and into our funny bones. He does this with all the subtlety of a B-1 bomber, as he takes on presidents, prime ministers and the front office of Major League Baseball, among other targets, in a fashion guaranteed to do no harm to any of them, except perhaps to cause them to laugh themselves to death.

Like many of the rest of us who come out of the African-American

Introduction

experience and are fortunate enough to have an avenue of expression in the major media, DeWayne Wickham strives to provide what Jesse Jackson calls "a voice for the voiceless," unbeholden to any interest but that of his readers and the improvement of our racially divided society.

The issues may be heavy, but the style is not ponderous. DeWayne's style reminds me of Toni Morrison's advice to writers: "The language must be careful and must appear effortless. It must not sweat. It must suggest and be provocative at the same time." You may not agree with everything DeWayne says, but you won't have any doubt as to where he stands.

And, he will make you think. That doesn't make him a bad person. It just means he's doing his job. "Those who profess to favor freedom, and yet deprecate agitation, are men who want crops without plowing up the ground," black journalist and freed slave Frederick Douglass said a century ago. "They want rain without thunder and lightning. They want the ocean without the awful roar of its many waters."

DeWayne's writings send forth a mighty roar. His truth shall make you free.

Clarence Page, *1989 Pulitzer Prize winner for commentary*

CHAPTER 1
Rogues, thugs and heroes

"All heroes, at bottom, die in vain, whether in war or in peace. The rewards of life go to those prudent enough to live on."

— H. L. Mencken

T was with more wit than wisdom that Mencken once uttered these words. Always the cynic, the man who came to be known as the Sage of Baltimore looked upon hero and villain alike with contempt.

For Mencken, as with most people, the line between hero and villain — the divide between doers of good deeds and the forces of evil — is sometimes so thin as to be indistinguishable.

A gallant revolutionary to some is a brutal terrorist to others. Oliver North was proclaimed a hero by Ronald Reagan and then found guilty by a jury of his peers. Both the president and the jurors came to their judgments after considering the Marine colonel's involvement in a plot to trade U.S. arms to Iran, in exchange for the release of American hostages being held by Islamic fundamentalists in Lebanon.

But for me, the line between hero and villain — more often than not — is about as wide as the ocean that divides the American and European continents. The more obvious of the rogues and thugs are people like "Flukey" Stokes and Al Sharpton, two men who profited from the pain of others.

Harder for some — though not me — to discern is the roguish behavior of Ronald Reagan and the thuggery of Mitch Snyder.

If, as Mencken suggests, true heroes die in vain, then the responsibility falls to the honest commentators among us to tout their good deeds and to hold up to public scorn the thugs and rogues who survive them. ■

Lousy retirement plan

KANSAS CITY, Mo., Dec. 3, 1986

Willie "Flukey" Stokes is dead. Good riddance!

An admitted gambler and convicted felon, Stokes was a reputed Chicago drug king whose garish lifestyle was believed financed by the pain and misery he peddled to junkies on the streets of the city's South Side.

"Chicago has lost one of its biggest sources of supply for cocaine and heroin," an official of the Drug Enforcement Administration was heard to remark shortly after Stokes was dispatched to his maker by a shotgun-toting assassin.

In life, Stokes was thought by some to be a "living legend" — his flamboyant lifestyle and evasion of the law having convinced many an impressionable person in Chicago's South Side ghetto that crime does pay. While he was arrested more than 70 times during his 49 years, Stokes was convicted just twice.

In death, he has become something of a folk hero to thousands of blacks, many of whom were among the more than 7,000 persons who stood in line for hours to attend Stokes' wake late last month. What a pity!

News of the death of Flukey Stokes came to me as I sat slumped in a waiting area of the Kansas City airport, my flight having been delayed more than an hour. It was for me the only bright spot in an otherwise miserable day.

For years Stokes had been the source of a regular flow of illegal drugs into the veins of Chicago junkies. He was the area's "major narcotics dealer," according to Richard Daley, Cook County state's attorney.

Stokes was known to strut about town in silk suits, with the arrogance of a man who defied police to prove him a liar for claiming that all of his riches came from gambling, and not the deadly sale of dope.

There are precious few black role models

There are precious few black role models in the inner cities of this nation. Integration and the aspirations of many middle-class blacks for "the good life" have caused these neighborhoods to be abandoned to people like Flukey Stokes.

in the inner cities of this nation. Integration and the aspirations of many middle-class blacks for "the good life" have caused these neighborhoods to be abandoned to people like Flukey Stokes.

In the process, millions of young blacks grow up watching honest, hard-working black men and women barely eke out a living working a 40-hour job, while the drug dealers among them flaunt their ill-gotten wealth. Little wonder that some of them opt for a life in the fast lane of the drug world.

It is worth noting that one of those young people so influenced was Stokes' 26-year-old son, Willie "The Wimp." The younger Stokes was thought to have been involved in a drug transaction back in 1984 when he was felled by a hail of bullets.

Willie "The Wimp" was put to rest in grand style. He was buried in a coffin made to resemble a Cadillac. Seated upright with his hands on the steering wheel, he wore a fedora and a red velvet suit. Between his fingers were $1,000 bills.

The funeral attracted 5,000 people and lots of national media attention.

In truth, it is often tough for the well-meaning among us to compete with the Flukey Stokes of the world for the hearts and minds of inner-city youths. What we have to offer them often falls far short of their materialistic goals. Not so the dope dealers.

Stokes had much to show for his life of crime. He owned three luxury cars and an expensive, albeit tasteless, wardrobe. He made regular gambling trips to Las Vegas, where it was nothing for him to drop $250,000 in a weekend.

Last year on the occasion of his 30th wedding anniversary, Stokes threw a $200,000 party at which he presented his wife with a nine-carat diamond ring. In return, she gave him a ring with 40 carats of diamonds and an emerald centerpiece.

More often than not what we have to offer inner-city youngsters are unemployment statistics that give them little hope of finding honest work or, for the lucky ones who land a job, an income that barely raises them above the poverty level.

That's why I took some small comfort in Flukey Stokes' untimely demise. His death and that of his son provide me with the most compelling argument that can be made against a drug-trafficking career.

The retirement plan is lousy!

Liberating Grenada

WASHINGTON, Feb. 25, 1986

The idea is not without precedent.

The year is 1989 and Ronald Wilson Reagan, former president of the United States of America, is proclaimed prime minister of the island nation of Grenada. Don't laugh, it could very well happen.

And if it does come to pass — I have my fingers crossed — he won't be the first American citizen to take charge of a country south of the border. It has happened at least twice since 1856.

Even before Reagan made his triumphant trip last week to the Caribbean island he liberated in October 1983 from the grip of communism — with the help of more than 6,000 U.S. soldiers, airmen and Marines — the American president was being praised by Grenada's black population.

"Daddy Reagan," as many of Grenada's 110,000 residents affectionately call the president, could have the run of the tiny island. His image was plastered on handbills, which dotted buildings and banana trees across the island's 21-mile length, shortly before he arrived.

The message they carried called upon Grenadians to come out and welcome the American president. More than half of Grenada's population turned out to welcome Reagan.

If memory fails you, what Reagan did to earn such adulation was to topple Grenada's leftist government, imprison its leaders, and make way for a democratically elected government. All this while only trying to rescue 300 American medical students who were stranded on the island in the fall of 1983 while Grenada's leaders fought among themselves for control of the government.

Hail the conquering hero!

No public opinion poll is needed to determine that Ronald Reagan has won the hearts and minds of most Grenadians. Many reportedly say he can retire to their island and become prime minister.

Back in 1856, a scoundrel by the name of William Walker left his native Tennessee and repaired to Nicaragua, where he set off a series of events that resulted in his becoming president of that Central American nation. His reign was ended by a firing squad.

Sixty years later, the U.S. set up a military government in the Dominican Republic under the rule of a Marine captain. It's uncertain just how long the captain was left in charge, but the U.S. military government was in power from 1916 until 1924.

Once installed, there's no telling how long Reagan would dominate the politics of Grenada. Hopefully, he would stay in power long enough to effect yet another liberation.

He could turn his attention to the plight of this nation's 24 million black citizens, a majority of whom suffer from a kind of oppression that is as unjust as that which made life so unbearable for the people of Grenada.

In the fashion of *The Mouse That Roared,* Reagan could lead an army of Grenadians into the American heartland to rescue blacks in this country from the far right-wing forces that view civil rights and communism with the same disdain.

He could topple those fiscal conservatives who believe that the federal budget should be balanced on the backs of this nation's poor and disenfranchised.

Reagan could then rout those in the U.S. government who are opposed to affirmative action, and imprison fifth columnists such as Clarence Pendleton, Clarence Thomas, Thomas Sowell and Walter Williams — just as while president he aided in jailing Grenada's misguided leaders.

Can you imagine Reagan making a triumphant visit to Harlem, Watts or Liberty City, as throngs of blacks line the streets shouting praise to him? Then, and probably only then, will blacks in this country come to embrace Ronald Reagan as Grenadians did last week.

Failing such a turn of events, the great liberator of Grenada will — in all likelihood — go down in history as the U.S. president most disliked by black Americans.

Familiarity, you see, breeds contempt.

Hero of Howard Beach

NEW YORK, June 6, 1988

To a lot of people in Howard Beach, Jon Lester is a hero.

Never mind that he was just sentenced to 30 years in jail for manslaughter, or that he is also serving time on conspiracy and handgun violation charges.

Rogues, thugs and heroes

Forget for the moment that the 18-year-old tough guy instigated a vicious assault on three blacks that left one man dead and another brutally beaten.

Ignore, if you will, the account of witnesses who testified in court that on the night of the attack Lester burst into a neighborhood party shouting: "There's niggers on the boulevard. Let's go kill them!" What is important for you to know, his friends contend, is that Jon Lester is a good white kid who is being persecuted by a handful of politicians and civil rights activists.

That's the message they were trying to get across when more than 1,500 residents of Howard Beach, a small neighborhood in the Queens section of New York, wrote the court recently pleading for leniency in the sentencing of Lester.

Obviously there are a lot of people in Howard Beach who find little fault in what Jon Lester did on the night of Dec. 20, 1986. What a pity!

By most accounts, Lester was the leader of a gang of white youths that attacked three black men who wandered into Howard Beach looking for help after their car broke down on a nearby expressway.

While one of the blacks sprinted to safety, the other two were beaten with tree branches and a baseball bat. One of them, 23-year-old Michael Griffith, was chased onto a roadway where he was struck and killed by a car.

"What greatly disturbs me" about Lester, the judge said before sentencing, is that after seeing Griffith killed, he pressed the attack against the other black man, beating him brutally with a baseball bat — an action for which "he shows no remorse, no sense of guilt, no shame, no fear."

But the judge saved his most biting criticism for the good people of Howard Beach, those who wrote him in defense of Lester and the racial attack he incited.

"What disturbs me about all these letters is that there is no remorse," the judge complained. "What happened in Howard Beach — and make no mistake about it, no ifs, ands or buts about it — it was a racial incident that triggered off the violence.

"What should be obvious to everyone here," he told the packed courtroom, "is that racism breeds hatred and hatred breeds racism and it is a vicious cycle." And so it is.

But even more, what should be most alarming about the attitudes of those who wrote in Lester's defense is that they are not alone. It seems that an increasingly large number of whites in this country believe that racial incidents are on the decline.

Like Lester's supporters, they believe that blacks and other minorities bring these attacks on themselves — that they provoke the violence of which they complain.

Most of these people are unmindful of the damage racial violence, and their condoning attitudes, do to the fabric of our nation. Little do they realize that most great societies are destroyed from within, and not by the forces that lurk outside their borders.

Unnoticed, or disbelieved, by these people was the recent study published by the National Council of Churches on hate violence in the United States.

"Not a day has passed in the last seven years without someone in the United States being victimized by hate violence," the study — which is titled *They Don't All Wear White Sheets* — reported.

"Harassment, vandalism, arson, assault and murder motivated by racism, anti-Semitism or other forms of bigotry — such as homophobia — plague every section of our country," the authors concluded.

Not surprisingly, among the incidents of hate violence cited in the 95-page report was the Howard Beach assault.

For what he did, Jon Lester will spend at least the next 10 years of his life in jail before he is eligible for parole.

But still at large are the warped attitudes of people — like those in Howard Beach who came to Lester's defense — that give rise to racial bigotry and violence.

No place for 'Frank's Place'

BALTIMORE, Oct. 12, 1988

There is something about what Kim LeMasters did that makes me think of Robert Irsay.

Irsay, you may remember, is the guy who waited until the dead of night to move the Baltimore Colts football team to Indianapolis — a blasphemous act that has earned him a place alongside Bela Lugosi as one of the nation's most outrageous body snatchers.

LeMasters is a villain of another sort.

As president of CBS Entertainment, he's the guy responsible for pulling the plug on *Frank's Place,* just one week before it was to go into production for a second season.

It didn't take me long to get over Baltimore's loss of the Colts. Memory of the season tickets I held faded quickly with the realization that the Irsay-led Indianapolis Colts have more in common with Jamaican bobsledders than the football teams that Johnny Unitas once led to victory.

But getting over the loss of *Frank's Place,* a television show in which the image of blacks regularly was raised above that of prostitutes, pimps and grown men with Mohegan haircuts, will take a lot longer.

Credit the creative success of the so-called dramedy — a show that is supposed to be both dramatic and funny — to its executive producers, Hugh Wilson and Tim Reid, two men who broke a lot of taboos by assembling one of the most racially integrated production teams in television. The program won three of the nine Emmys for which it was nominated earlier this year.

But, as just about any television executive with a desire to stay in the business will tell you, it is rating points and not the review of critics that keep shows on the air. And when it came to ratings, this show was in trouble from the start.

"Frank's Place embodied every element of excellence that a programmer would want to see in a television show," LeMasters said the other day after canceling production of the 13 new episodes CBS ordered back in May.

"It received the widespread support of CBS, of television critics and a broad spectrum of the entertainment community," he added. "Unfortunately, the viewing audience failed to respond to it." Thanks to the CBS scheduling wizards, gauging audience response to *Frank's Place* was not an easy task. From its debut last fall to the show's final airing earlier this month, CBS bounced *Frank's Place* through six time slots over three days — a network game of hide-and-seek that stripped the show of all but its most devout followers. And that's too bad.

Frank's Place was a cultural achievement that is unmatched in American television history. For the short span of one television season, it did more to correct decades of media caricatures of blacks than any other program on TV, including the much celebrated *Cosby Show.*

It was a program about as soulful as a mouthful of collard greens, but one that did not reek of the ethnic banter and jive talk that has too often been used by television producers to symbolize their black characters.

Frank's Place was a show that caused viewers to laugh mostly *with* its characters, and not *at* them as so many programs with black casts — and racially insensitive producers — do.

For a good number of television viewers who were starved for real-life portrayals of blacks, *Frank's Place* came the closest to meeting the challenge.

It was real in its portrayal of a black high school athlete who was pursued by scores of college recruiters — men who measure the young man only by what he accomplished on the basketball court, not on an SAT exam.

The show was real when it handled subjects like drug abuse, voodoo and homelessness.

And real in the way it dealt with the super-sensitive issue of discrimination among blacks.

Where else on television today are you going to see a program deal effectively with this issue, which is largely invisible to most whites? "All my life I've been the only black," Frank confides to a friend who invites him to join an exclusive club for fair-skin blacks, despite his darker complexion.

"I was the only black in this class. I was the only black in that organization. I was the only black on this team. But, I've got to tell ya, man, I'm not about to be the only black in a black club! That's going a little too far, don't ya think?"

Well, nobody is about to accuse LeMasters of going too far with *Frank's Place*.

More likely, his name will find its way onto a list, with that of Robert Irsay, of those who broke and ran in spots where more courageous people would have stood their ground — at least for one more season.

A not-so-good Samaritan

WASHINGTON, March 28, 1989

Mitch Snyder demanded his day in court. He insisted that the Supreme Court hear his case. Snyder wants desperately to win. I hope he loses.

A professional advocate for this city's homeless population, Snyder hustles his concern for the poor in much the same way that pimps care for their whores. The attention he gives them is born more of self-interest than human compassion.

There may have been a time when Snyder walked in the shadow of Mother Teresa, but now it seems he is transfixed by the glow from television cameras and the even brighter lights of Hollywood movie makers.

A nationally known advocate of the poor, Snyder also has locked arms with a host of Fortune 500 firms — which have filed briefs in support of him — in his fight to make good a claim to the copyright of an artwork that was created by someone else.

Three years ago, Snyder's organization, The Community For Creative Non-Violence, commissioned a sculptor to fashion the life-size images of a homeless family sitting atop a steam grate, an image that Snyder said is the creation of his mind's eye, if not his physical handiwork.

The artwork, which is titled *Third World America*, was to be a visual reminder of the suffering of this nation's homeless people — and its copyright belongs to Snyder, his lawyers contend.

Snyder says the $15,000 he shelled out for the sculpture also bought him the artwork's copyright. James Earl Reid, the work's sculptor, who says he did the job at cost out of sympathy for Snyder's cause, disagrees.

Inside the Supreme Court this week, lawyers for Snyder — whose efforts on behalf of Washington's homeless gained him national attention when actor Martin Sheen portrayed him in a 1986 television movie — stood before the bench and argued their client's case.

Nearby, another team of lawyers huddled around Reid, the Baltimore man whose hands created the sculpture that has given rise to this benchmark legal case. Himself a struggling artist, Reid is likely to find immortality in this nation's law journals, regardless of how the court rules. To legal purists, the issues in this case are just that important.

But to me and millions of others whose attention span shrinks noticeably whenever lawyers open their mouths, the only thing interesting about Community For Creative Non-Violence vs. James Earl Reid is the soap opera plot. This case has to be a dream come true of tabloid headline writers: "Poor Advocate Claims Poverty Copyright" or "Homeless Crusader's Immaculate Conception." It is also the kind of story line that is likely to elevate Snyder's celebrity status a notch or two — maybe enough to earn him a book contract or Hollywood movie deal.

A white liberal activist whose trademark is a neatly pressed army fatigue jacket that makes him look more like a member of Cuba's aging revolution than a leader of Washington's overwhelmingly black homeless, Snyder shows less interest in the legal issues of this landmark case than the media attention it is generating.

As lawyers for the two men argued before the Supreme Court, Snyder was on the street outside, standing next to the contested sculpture he moved there for the day. Inside the high court were lawyers and their legal arguments. Outside were Snyder and the television and newspaper cameras.

Somewhere along the way to finding housing for the homeless, Mitch Snyder became a media celebrity. It was a bumpy road that began 17 years ago when Snyder walked out on his wife and two sons in New York in search of a better life for himself.

While his family survived on welfare payments and food stamps, Snyder — a former washing machine salesman — surfaced in Washington as a champion of this city's homeless and poor. For 13 years, he had no contact with the family he deserted. When his ex-wife heard that he was to be the subject of a TV movie — ironically titled, *Samaritan: The Mitch Snyder Story* — for which he would be paid $150,000, she called to ask him to help with his sons' education. Snyder's ex-wife said in a recent newspaper interview that he promised to send a few hundred dollars. Nice guy, huh? And now, this former "Maytag Man of the Month" has gone to court to wrest the copyright for an artwork that symbolizes the oppression of poor people from its struggling creator.

"I don't consider myself a good person," Snyder confessed to a reporter earlier this year.

All things considered, I couldn't agree more.

A second-story man

NEW YORK, March 29, 1988

Mention Tawana Brawley here and the talk quickly turns to Al Sharpton.

Brawley is the black teen-ager whose story of abduction and rape by six white men last November has turned into an ugly legal standoff between her lawyers and state prosecutors.

Sharpton is responsible for a good bit of the ugliness associated with this case.

A black evangelist and FBI informant, Sharpton is a crafty manipulator who craves the media spotlight in much the same way that second-story men delight in an open window.

The open window for him in this case was created by Brawley's attorneys, C. Vernon Mason and Alton Maddox Jr., who allowed Sharpton to finagle his way into their confidence and that of Brawley's family — a decision that certainly hurts the credibility of their efforts.

In representing the 16-year-old Brawley, who was found Nov. 28 in a plastic bag near Poughkeepsie with dog feces in her hair and the word "nigger" scrawled on her body, the attorneys have thus far refused to allow her to cooperate with state investigators.

By doing so they are seeking to dictate the course of the investigation, a strategy the two men used successfully in representing the victims of the 1986 racial attack in Howard Beach. Their charges of "cover-up" in that case resulted in the appointment of a special prosecutor of their liking and the eventual conviction of several of the white youths arrested for the assault that left one black man dead and another severely beaten.

Then, Sharpton was a leader of protesting blacks. He hovered outside the courtroom and in front of television cameras throughout much of the Howard Beach trial. His critics within the black community say he was more concerned with pumping his image than in the outcome of the case. It is a charge that is not without merit.

According to leaked federal government documents and reports in *Newsday* and *The Village Voice,* the portly preacher is a con man and hustler who has spent much of the past decade consorting with world-class thugs, while spying on black politicians and activists for the FBI. Sharpton's denials of the accusations are not convincing.

Since involving himself in the Brawley case, Sharpton has compared New York Attorney General Robert Abrams to Adolf Hitler. He also has charged that the black teen-ager's attackers included members of the Dutchess County sheriff's office and a county prosecutor — a thus far unsubstantiated charge that seems to be part of the legal strategy of Mason and Maddox.

But a strategy bent upon discrediting prosecutors and police investigators who may lack the zeal for pursuing the Brawley case is one that is fraught with a lot of dangers. Not the least of which is the backlash that comes from blacks who believe Brawley's rape charge and want her assailants brought to justice.

They are growing increasingly impatient with the delaying tactics of Maddox and Mason and their refusal to let Brawley appear before a grand jury or talk to investigators from Abrams' office.

And as bits and pieces of information that seem to poke holes in Brawley's story surface, public opinion appears to be shifting. Nearly all of the blacks with whom I spoke while in New York recently now doubt Brawley's version of the events surrounding her four-day disappearance.

"This thing just started to come apart when Al Sharpton got involved," one woman complained.

"Everybody knows how sleazy he is," she said. And then, pausing for a moment, conceded: "Well, almost everybody."

Obviously attorneys C. Vernon Mason and Alton Maddox Jr. don't know, or don't care much about, what nearly everyone else knows about Sharpton.

The last thing they need is to allow Sharpton to seize the media spotlight in the Brawley case.

What they should understand is that a good second-story man doesn't need much of an opening to rip off the unsuspecting.

Reluctant hero

WASHINGTON, Dec. 21, 1988

Max Robinson never wanted to be anybody's role model. But in both life and death he came to symbolize much that is important to millions of us.

For the better part of his 20-year career as a broadcast journalist, Robinson was a draftee in the social conflict that sprang from the civil rights movement — a conscript in our battles to overcome racism and discrimination.

He began his journalism career in earnest in 1965, near the bottom of his craft, as a floor director at a television station here in Washington — a job that sometimes required him to sweep floors. Four years later when he became co-anchor of the station's evening news, his name was added to the list of "black firsts" that serves as an awkward benchmark of the progress blacks make in this country.

Jackie Robinson, the first black to play in major league baseball.

Benjamin O. Davis Sr., the first black general officer in the U.S. military.

Shirley Chisholm, the first black woman elected to Congress.

Max Robinson, the first black to anchor a local newscast in a major television market.

It was the kind of notice that made Robinson uncomfortable.

When he died Tuesday, having lost his quiet battle with AIDS, many of his peers began rummaging through the record of his life, looking for something to say about this man who in 1978 became the first black network news anchor.

Some of them called him a legend. Others, less compassionate, talked about his bouts with depression and his drinking problem — the kind of things that cut role models down a notch or two. But then that's OK, because Robinson never wanted to be anybody's role model.

All he ever wanted was to practice his craft without the public attention and celebrity status that came with all of his firsts.

"I felt a tremendous amount of pressure when I took this job that I could not fail," he said shortly after landing the anchoring job with ABC News. "And that kind of burden is much too great for anybody to have to carry. To constantly be guarding against failure, almost guarantees failure."

Failure was Robinson's greatest fear.

We all tended to heap a lot of burdens on Robinson's broad shoulders. When a group of us got together here 13 years ago to form the National Association of Black Journalists, we knew that our success depended on our ability to get some media celebrities to embrace the idea.

Robinson attended the meeting and agreed to become a founding member, but he turned down an opportunity to assume a leadership role in the organization.

Last August, the group gave the ailing Robinson its "President's Award" in recognition of his outstanding contributions to the profession. Translated, that means we thanked him for being the unwitting point man in our struggle for wider inclusion of blacks in the media. Frail and weakened by the effects of AIDS, he stood proud and erect before the more than 1,300 black journalists who assembled for the occasion to see him accept the award.

A few months later, in his last public appearance, Robinson offered this advice to students at Howard University. "Try to keep your integrity," he said, "because you'll find out in life, at the end, that's all you've got."

And it was his sense of integrity that moved Robinson to allow his family to reveal his bout with AIDS shortly after his death. He "expressed the desire that his death be the occasion for emphasizing the importance, particularly to the black community, of education about AIDS and methods of its prevention," family members said in a written statement. "He hoped that people would recognize the urgency of developing effective treatments for the disease and more humane policies toward its victims." Even in death, Robinson felt compelled to shoulder yet another burden for others.

More than a role model, Max Robinson is an American hero in a profession that is not well-known for its good guys.

When an apology falls short

WASHINGTON, May 9, 1988

There are times when an apology just isn't enough to right an ugly wrong.

Steve Cokely tried to quiet the many people he offended in Chicago recently by scribbling a few words of apology on a piece of paper. But it was hardly enough to quell the protest or save his job as an aide to acting Mayor Eugene Sawyer.

Having publicly accused Jewish doctors of causing the AIDS epi-

Rogues, thugs and heroes

demic by injecting the virus into blacks, Cokely was also heard to say that black children are made to attend school so that whites can profit from the inoculations they are required to get.

Not done, he labeled Christopher Columbus a "Hispanic Jew" and blasted Jesse Jackson for having Jewish advisers.

Then, when it appeared that public outrage over his remarks imperiled his $36,000-a-year city job, Cokely began to moonwalk on his convictions.

Saying he "humbly apologizes," the black mayoral aide clung to his city paycheck while Mayor Sawyer waffled in reaction to Cokely's bigotry.

"He's got a wife and family; he needs the income," Sawyer offered lamely in defense of his initial reluctance to jettison Cokely from the municipal payroll.

"What Steve Cokely does on his own time ... is his business," the mayor's press secretary said while his boss was explaining that Cokely "indicated to me that he did not mean those things in his heart."

In the end, Sawyer succumbed to public pressure, if not good sense, and fired his community liaison aide.

But in next year's mayoral election, Sawyer will no doubt be called on to explain why he didn't rid his administration of Cokely with the dispatch that Mike Tyson floors his boxing opponents. And rightfully so.

Likewise, many voters in New York can be expected to remember the bigotry of Ed Koch when next they go to the polls to elect a mayor.

It was Koch who spewed his racist venom throughout The Big Apple during last month's New York presidential primary.

Saying "Jews would be crazy" to vote for Jesse Jackson, Koch lashed out at the black presidential contender with the kind of rage that Eugene "Bull" Connor once vented upon defenseless civil rights protesters.

Citing disputes over Jackson's 20-year-old claim that he was the last to speak to Martin Luther King Jr. in the moments after he was struck down by an assassin's bullet and the candidate's initial refusal to acknowledge his 1984 "Hymietown" remark, Koch called the black Baptist minister a liar.

The feisty mayor also charged that, if elected, Jackson would bankrupt the nation with his domestic policy proposals — ideas that have won the overwhelming support of black voters.

Given the Democratic mayor's ruptured relations with blacks in New York, his critics had good reason to suggest that his attacks on Jackson were racially inspired.

Ironically, Koch is now making overtures to blacks, who along with Hispanics, hold the key to his expected 1989 re-election bid. The two groups are thought to comprise a majority of Democratic Party voters in New York — a city that has been rife with racial incidents in recent years.

Sensing the rage engendered among blacks in his city, Koch too has shown a willingness to backtrack on his convictions in order to save his job.

"I'm sorry that I injured their feelings," Koch said of the black voters he must go before next year. "And I will try to redress that as best I can, not just with words, but with programs," the mayor told reporters.

And what kind of programs will he be offering disillusioned blacks? Koch says he's talking about new city-funded housing and health programs in poor neighborhoods. That sounds like the kind of domestic programs "hizzoner" once said Jackson would use to bankrupt America.

"I regret any pain I may have caused the supporters of Jesse Jackson," Koch offered after the New York primary. "It may be I didn't take into consideration sufficiently the impact of the criticism."

Yeah. And it just may be that next year New York voters will teach Ed Koch the lesson Steve Cokely had to learn the hard way: There are times when an apology just isn't enough to right an ugly wrong.

A broken heart

ATLANTA, Nov. 23, 1987

It's been a long time between headlines for Ross Barnett.

Twenty-five years ago Barnett made front-page news when he took on the federal courts and the president of the United States in his attempt to block the desegregation of the University of Mississippi.

Barnett stood shoulder to shoulder with people like George Wallace, Lester Maddox and Bull Connor — men who loosed the rage of Southern bigots on people who agitated for racial integration and the civil

Rogues, thugs and heroes

rights of blacks.

He would "rot in jail" rather than allow blacks to "ever darken the sacred threshold of our white schools," the former Mississippi governor told his supporters during the height of his confrontation with federal authorities. But in the end, blacks were allowed to attend Ole Miss and Barnett spent years beating back the efforts of federal prosecutors to jail him for his actions.

Last week Barnett was in the news again. This time he made the obituary page. The notice of his passing in this city's Sunday newspaper made no mention of the cause of death, but I suspect he died of a broken heart.

While the South of today is far from utopia for blacks, it bears no resemblance to the racially polarized region that Barnett shared in governing. Where once mean-spirited segregationists dominated the politics of the old Confederacy, there now exists a new political order — one that is more tolerant of the goals and aspirations of blacks. It is this kind of racial progress that surely must have first caused Barnett's brittle heart to crack.

In the years since he left the political stage, hundreds of blacks have won election to offices throughout the South. Atlanta, New Orleans, Birmingham, Little Rock and Richmond now have black mayors. The city manager of Dallas is black. And in Charlotte, where the city's black mayor lost his re-election bid earlier this month to a white woman, the major campaign issue was traffic congestion, not race. It all had to be too much for Barnett's old ticker.

While other segregationists, like Wallace and Strom Thurmond, seemed to have made their peace with the changing times, Barnett was quoted several years after leaving public office as saying about his actions as governor: "Generally speaking, I'd do it all over again."

Given that attitude, Barnett's heart must have begun to rupture badly last year when Michael Espy won election to Congress from Mississippi. A bright young lawyer, Espy is the first black to represent the state in Congress since Reconstruction. When Espy's victory was announced, the cracking of Barnett's segregationist heart must have been heard around the state.

Most people who remember this white supremacist in his glory days understand that his heart surely was taxed heavily by the Senate's recent rejection of Supreme Court nominee Robert Bork — a defeat made possible by conservative Southern senators who voted against President Reagan's nominee for fear of losing the support of their black constituents.

Can you imagine how this must have pained Barnett, who once said of blacks: "The Negro is different because God made him different to punish him."

We all must die someday and I guess Barnett preferred that his end came when it did. He probably couldn't stand the thought of living through next year's presidential campaign and looking on as Jesse Jackson, a black preacher from Greenville, S.C., wins the lion's share of delegates in Southern states.

There is not much left these days of old racists like Ross Barnett, except for an occasional confrontation — public clashes in places such as Forsyth County, Ga., or in the Howard Beach neighborhood of New York.

Today's racism is much too subtle for his style. Where once he and others stood tall in their public opposition to the advancement of blacks, the bigots of today are wimps by comparison. They are more intellectual terrorists than foot soldiers of white supremacy.

I don't know what the doctors will say was the cause of his death, but it's clear to me that Ross Barnett's heart was under more pressure than it could possibly stand.

CHAPTER 2
No justice, just us!

COMEDIAN Richard Pryor has a routine in which he says that this nation's court system is stacked against blacks:

"You go down there looking for justice, that's what you'll find, just us!"

In fact, for many black Americans, the scales of justice are heavily out of balance. Jails and prisons in this country have become just another urban ghetto, one in which black men largely are locked into a life of hopelessness. The prison system is the American gulag, a warehouse for the human spirit, more than a lockup for the criminal element.

And while thousands of blacks swell the population of this country's penal system, there are those among us — both black and white — whose bodies are free, but whose minds are committed to a solitary confinement. The weight of their jaundiced views adds to the imbalance, legal and otherwise, that blacks are made to suffer.

In truth, Pryor is right. Justice for many blacks is the most elusive part of the American dream. Those who end up behind bars are just the most obvious evidence of this reality.

But any system that denies a people justice is hard-pressed to contain such fascist behavior to a single segment of society. Nearly every black who has aspired to opportunity has known the pain and frustration that comes with justice denied. Anyone who has ever been called "nigger," or treated like one, understands the humiliation and rage this racial disrespect generates.

In one way or another, most black Americans are forced almost daily to confront the limits of this nation's egalitarianism. Whether it is the actions of a largely segregated media, or simply the warped thoughts of men who are desperately in search for someone to blame among the victims of American racism, Pryor's words represent a chilling reality for far too many blacks. ■

Journalistic wilding

WASHINGTON, May 17, 1989

They called it "wilding." That's the label the New York media used to describe the actions of the teen-age gang that brutally beat and raped a jogger in Central Park last month.

There are hundreds of rapes in New York each year, but this was one that captured the attention of people across the country.

The victim was a lone female jogger who took a late-night run through Central Park. Her attackers, police said, are teen-agers — some as young as 14. They went to the park that night intent upon raising hell.

And there is another important ingredient to this story. The 28-year-old victim is white. Those who brutalized her are black.

Almost every day since the April 20 attack, newspapers in New York have wallowed in this story. Several national publications, including *Time*, *Newsweek* and *People* magazines, have devoted space to this sexual assault. And just this week ABC's *Nightline* waded into the coverage.

Rape — any rape — is a heinous crime. But the rape of white women by blacks always seems to evoke a greater outpouring of rage and anguish from people in this country.

Ironically, days before the white jogger was attacked in Central Park, a black woman was raped by two black men atop a high-rise apartment in Harlem and then thrown from the 21-story building.

She broke her fall by grabbing hold of some cable TV wires outside an 18th-floor window. Naked and badly bruised, the woman hung on until rescued by a building resident.

Not surprisingly, the report of her harrowing experience got scant coverage from New York media.

Rape — any rape — is a heinous crime. But the rape of white women by blacks always seems to evoke a greater outpouring of rage and anguish from people in this country.

Two weeks after the attack on the white jogger, a black woman in Brooklyn was forced to an apartment rooftop, raped by three black men, and then thrown down an air shaft. Despite being hospitalized in critical condition, her story drew little attention from a New York press corps that was still giving front-page coverage to the jogging victim.

The media's preoccupation with this white rape victim is no mere chance. Sexual crimes committed by black men against white women — both real and perceived — often have given rise to mob action on the part of white men and the media they control.

Nearly a third of all black men lynched this century were accused of raping white women. And throughout this period, media organizations — particularly newspapers — have shown a rabid interest in the alleged crimes. Those of the accused black men that is, not the white mobs.

Worse yet, the crimes of whites who rape blacks go largely unnoticed by media organizations and are devalued by the criminal justice system. Take the example of Joanne Little.

When Little was raped in her jail cell by a white policeman in 1975, it was left largely to the black press and activist community to keep her story before the public.

Ironically, North Carolina prosecutors tried Little for killing her attacker, despite finding his naked body — and other evidence of the sexual assault — in her cell.

"The American rape complex was productive of much injustice," historians Mary Frances Berry and John Blassingame wrote in their book *Long Memory.*

Back in 1951, Matt Ingram stood on a North Carolina street and admired the shapely form of a young white woman walking nearby. He uttered not a single word, but it didn't matter. Charged with "rape by leer," the black sharecropper was found guilty and sent to prison.

Four years later, 14-year-old Emmett Till whistled at a white woman in Money, Miss. For this "crime," he was kidnapped and savagely murdered by members of a white mob.

Up until 1977, when the Supreme Court ruled unconstitutional the death penalty in rape cases, scores of black men were sentenced to die for sexually assaulting white women. But when asked the number of whites who got the death penalty for raping black women prior to the high court's decision, an official of the NAACP Legal Defense Fund — an organization that tracks death row inmates — answered dryly: "I don't know of a single case."

As repulsive as it was, the rape of the white jogger in Central Park is no more demanding of justice — or media attention — than the brutal attacks upon the two black women who were raped and then thrown from the tops of buildings.

Those news organizations that think otherwise are guilty of journalistic "wilding."

Robed scoundrels

MIAMI, Oct. 13, 1987

The people who are trying to lynch Alcee Hastings all wear robes. But unlike the cowardly Klansmen who drape themselves in white sheets to disguise their identities, though not their purpose, Hastings' attackers go about proudly in the black gowns of federal judges.

They differ from the Ku Kluxers not only in the color of their cloaks, but also in the courage of their conviction. Few of them are willing to state honestly their objections to the man, Florida's first black federal judge.

Last week Hastings flew to Washington to pick up a copy of the charges lodged against him by some of his colleagues on the federal bench — judges who have asked Congress to impeach the outspoken black jurist.

Hastings has been accused of conspiring with a prominent Washington lawyer to solicit a bribe from two convicted racketeers.

William Borders, the accused lawyer, was himself convicted in a separate trial on charges of conspiring to arrange a bribe.

If all of this has a familiar ring, it is because the case first drew national media attention back in 1983 when a federal jury acquitted Hastings of the criminal charges in this case.

And so why is he now facing possible impeachment? Because some of his judicial colleagues say they believe the evidence that was presented against Hastings.

Sound like double jeopardy? Not to the five-judge appeals court panel that concluded there was "clear and convincing evidence" of Hastings' guilt, his jury acquittal notwithstanding.

Leaning heavily on a 1980 law that allows members of the judiciary to discipline their own, the judges are determined to accomplish what federal prosecutors could not: the removal of Alcee Hastings from office.

They argue that impeachment is not a criminal prosecution, and therefore does not constitute double jeopardy in this case. While they may have the letter of the law on their side, they are far afield of its spirit.

It is hard to imagine that Congress intended for this law to be used to overturn a jury decision — something the judges seem determined to do. More likely, what members of Congress had in mind when they enacted the legislation was to provide the judiciary with a means of disciplining members of the bench as an alternative to criminal proceedings.

But this judicial abuse has not sapped the fight from Hastings.

"If I committed perjury, they should bring criminal charges," he said angrily, suggesting that his accusers are unwilling to submit what evidence they have to another federal jury.

"All they have is the same evidence that was either used, or available for use" by federal prosecutors in the 1983 trial, Hastings charged.

In fact, the judges had sought to keep their charges against Hastings secret, refusing even to provide the embattled black judge with a copy. That's the kind of justice one expects in Siberia, not Washington.

At Hastings' urging, Congress voted last week to make public the 301-page document.

Throughout this legal ordeal, Hastings has spent more than $167,000, "including my mother's Social Security money," on his defense. Of this sum, $60,000 has been spent since his 1983 acquittal, the judge said.

Now Alcee Hastings faces impeachment on the charges that forced him to undergo a jury trial. Why? Some suggest it is happening because he is black. Others say it is because of his arrogance. I suspect both have something to do with it.

"Alcee Hastings is his own worst enemy," a black federal judge told me in a whispered conversation. "He has always taken pleasure in tweaking the noses of his enemies, and now they are paying him back." It's been six years now since the initial charges were brought against

Hastings, four years since he was acquitted, and still he is under attack.

"We really are in high cotton on this issue," Hastings said, referring to the serious legal questions involved in his case.

"The best thing I can do to keep my balance is to make this both my job and pain," the black judge said.

As he waits for Congress to decide his fate, there are no other options for him.

Brothers

CHICAGO, May 5, 1987

It was an awesome sight.

From inside a car hurtling along the Dan Ryan Expressway at 55 miles per hour, the long line of 16-story buildings hovered over the roadway with a menacing presence.

Two miles in length, the 28 structures of the Robert Taylor Homes — Chicago's largest public housing project — contrast with the wealthy neighborhoods of the city's nearby lakefront much like Soweto does to Johannesburg.

And like the South African township, the Robert Taylor Homes is more a human warehouse than a place where blacks would willingly choose to raise their families. It is an inner-city jungle in which only the truly strong survive, a microcosm of black urban America that has been largely unrevealed to white America.

Last week, *Newsweek* magazine peered into the graffiti-stained buildings of the Robert Taylor Homes, and into the lives of 12 black men — men whose lives once merged in this Chicago housing project.

The 27-page cover story, called simply *Brothers,* was a foray into a world in which deferred dreams and dashed hopes have a cancerous effect on the inhabitants. A world in which success is measured in terms of one's ability just to survive. A world in which most people fear what tomorrow will bring.

Reported by four black journalists, one of whom grew up in the Robert Taylor Homes, the story offered readers an understanding of life in this ghetto that no white journalist could have captured. In many ways their reporting was autobiographical — a mirror image of what black men and women experience in urban ghettos across this nation.

"We just wanted to put something honest out there," Sylvester Monroe was overheard to explain shortly after the magazine hit the streets last week. It was Monroe, who grew up in the Robert Taylor Homes, who convinced his editors at *Newsweek* to take on the story.

"We wanted to humanize all of the statistics that we were getting about black men," Monroe Anderson, another of the *Newsweek* correspondents who worked on the article, told me. "The guys we reported on aren't stereotypes. They are people with dreams and ambitions. They aren't all bad, or all good. But they are all real people." They are also America's "invisible men," people whose existence this society largely has failed to acknowledge. They are the men census takers seldom count — men unemployment statistics never pick up.

It has always been much easier for white Americans to believe "they" don't exist, that is unless and until "they" emerge from their ghettos. Most come out full of anger and rage. Some, who run afoul of the law, are quickly dispatched to jail — that other black ghetto. A few, like Sylvester Monroe, get lucky and escape relatively unscathed.

The Chicago men, whose life stories *Newsweek* offered to its readers, have nicknames like Half Moon, Hook and Pee Wee. But they could just as easily be Frog, Pissy and Jitters — black men who grew up with me in a Baltimore public housing project.

I called an old friend, a man I hadn't talked to for several years, soon after I read the article to find out if he had seen it. We talked for hours about what it was like for us growing up in the projects.

"There were a lot of guys who didn't make it out of Cherry Hill," he said of those we left behind in that Baltimore housing project.

Yeah, but there were also a good number of us who got out. And that's what struck me as being so important about the *Newsweek* article.

It is not just another story about the failures of blacks. It is a revealing look at a slice of life in black America that is both personal and honest — a glimpse of what it is like growing up black in an urban ghetto, offered from a unique perspective.

"Through portraits of our lives together and apart, I thought, we might find some answers as to why black men in America seem almost an endangered species," Sylvester Monroe wrote in the article's prologue.

Probably not. But what he, and his colleagues, did accomplish was no less impressive.

They have, if only for the moment, put the plight of the black poor back onto the national agenda.

About William Raspberry and Red Adair

WASHINGTON, June 4, 1988

The odds are William Raspberry has never talked to Paul "Red" Adair.

It's a good bet that no one who believes they can use "bucket brigades" to extinguish a firestorm has ever taken counsel from Adair, a man well known for his ability to douse an inferno.

Raspberry, a syndicated columnist with *The Washington Post,* offered blacks some firefighting advice recently — the kind of advice that if taken seriously could cause the unsuspecting to go up in flames.

"Black America's house is on fire," Raspberry wrote in a recent column intended to sound the alarm. The evidence of this conflagration, the black columnist said, "is plain to see."

And just who is it that has torched black America?

If you answered the racists among us — those who make continued efforts to deny blacks access to opportunities — Raspberry says you are wrong. Oh, he admits that racism is still a problem for blacks, but he says black Americans are their own worst enemy.

What is his evidence?

Raspberry points to a long list of social problems that plague black communities across the nation — births to unwed mothers, the illegal drug trade, poor academic achievement and black-on-black crime — as proof of his assertions that blacks have set ablaze their own house. The man obviously has smoke in his eyes.

Such an assessment suggests that: 1. Raspberry does not understand the difference between cause and effect; 2. He is unaware of the successful efforts being made by blacks to stem many of these problems.

"We are obsessed with the search for racist arsonists when our time would be far better spent forming bucket brigades to douse the flames," Raspberry argues.

Fire at will

But when it comes to firefighting, I'm sure Red Adair would agree that you can't extinguish a firestorm with buckets of water. It takes a lot more to cap an inferno at its source.

The source for most of these problems cannot be found within black communities. Of course, this doesn't mean that blacks have no obligation to work to improve their own condition. They most certainly do. But in fact blacks have been doing just that, in one way or another, for more than 350 years.

In recent years the intervention efforts of more than a score of black organizations have caused the teen-age pregnancy rate among black women to decline, even as it is increasing among whites.

In 1985, the National Urban League and the NAACP convened a meeting of black groups to address many of the problems that confront the black family — a meeting that has given rise to new outreach efforts among these organizations.

Black self-help should also be credited for the increased educational achievement of black students. The number of blacks graduating from high school rose from 67.5 percent in 1976 to 75.6 percent in 1985. And while only 18 percent of college-bound blacks attend historically black colleges, these schools account for 40 percent of all black degree holders — a less obvious form of self-help among blacks.

Black Americans also have shown a real willingness to help pay the cost of efforts to help themselves.

Charitable giving among blacks, as a percentage of their income, equals that of whites in this country in nearly every income category, according to a recent study by the Joint Center for Political Studies. Most of the dollars blacks donate go to charitable organizations within their communities — organizations that are pouring water on the fire that ravages black America.

Extinguishing the kind of gas- and oil-well fires that Red Adair is often called upon to fight is a real challenge. But throwing water on them amounts to little more than damage control. To snuff out these blazes requires a lot more effort.

And so it is with the flames that engulf black America.

Stemming the illegal drug trade and the rampant violence it gives rise to is not something blacks can do alone. The dons of cocaine are an international lot who are given aid and comfort by unscrupulous politicians and law enforcement officials. Extinguishing the fire they set requires a national solution.

Further reductions in the pregnancy rate among black teen-agers will come with time as self-help efforts in this area continue, just as progress is being made in the educational achievement of blacks.

But the fire Raspberry speaks of will continue to burn until America finds a way to extinguish the racism and lack of economic opportunity that spark this blaze.

Not a bigot

WASHINGTON, Sept. 16, 1986

Royce Mossholder says that he is not a racist, and I'm willing to accept that. But he is obviously a man troubled by his beliefs.

A regular reader of my column, he wrote me recently to express a view of blacks that he says is shared by millions of white Americans. Put simply, he feels that blacks contribute little, and take much, from the world in which we live.

By his own description, Mossholder is a "middle-aged, college grad, upper-income white male, from a lower-class background in the Midwest" who is made angry by the efforts of blacks to push their way into the American mainstream.

Mossholder's frustrations and bitterness spewed from his letter with the force of the blood that flows from the bodies of black South African children who challenge the oppressive rule of that nation's white-minority government. Listen.

"I am taking the time to write so that you may know that millions of Americans are like myself. We are not rednecks, we have been fair and we think generous, but we are fed up with blacks whining, begging, demanding. On and on it goes, every black shortcoming or failure blamed on racism," Mossholder wrote.

He said that blacks have caused a decline in "educational quality" in this country. And blacks, he charged, have contributed nothing "to the progress of mankind in raising itself above the level of Stone Age man" anywhere in the world — a failing, he says, that is particularly noticeable in Southern Africa.

"In short, I can look around the world, and I can see no place where blacks have accomplished anything," he complained.

Mossholder's letter rubbed me raw. My first instinct was to do as he suggested I might and toss it in the trash — to simply dismiss it as the rantings of a rabid racist.

But I was troubled by his assertion that "millions of Americans are like myself." I had to talk to him.

After a little effort I was able to get him on the phone. Much to my surprise he did not speak with the shrillness of a Klansman. His tone was conciliatory.

Mossholder told me that he exaggerated a bit in his letter to make his point, but maintained his belief that blacks offer little and take much from society.

"I don't know what to do about stereotypes," he said to me, "but I have a feeling that stereotypes are earned." But in fact they are created. And once done they are perpetuated by people like Royce Mossholder, whose myopic view of the world makes it difficult for him to separate myth from reality. What a shame.

America is today very much as it was in 1968 when the Kerner Commission issued its now famous report, two nations: one black, and the other white. The distance these largely segregated societies create between blacks and whites gives rise to our conflict, and I suspect, Mossholder's myopia.

He looks at affirmative action and set-aside programs and he sees blacks being guaranteed opportunities at the expense of whites. Unnoticed by him is the reality that a 10 percent set-aside for minorities leaves 90 percent guaranteed to whites.

He complains that the presence of blacks in America's public school system has caused a deterioration of "educational quality." That's the kind of narrow-mindedness we heard after World War II when the G.I. Bill opened up higher education to millions of white men from working-class families for the first time — people like Royce Mossholder.

And he cautions that "sooner or later" blacks will have to learn to row their "own boat," unmindful of the 250 years blacks spent shackled to the oars of white America's boat. He apparently is unaware that millions of unemployed blacks search daily without success for jobs, not handouts.

He thinks disparagingly of blacks who receive welfare assistance. But he probably gives little thought to the subsidies (for many, a less offensive form of public assistance) this nation gives to farmers, most of whom are white.

Mossholder says he is not a bigot, but rather a man who is simply fed up with the demands that blacks make of America. And he says that there are millions of other white people in this country who think as he does.

I wonder.

The wrong man

BALTIMORE, April 5, 1987

How much is 10 years of a person's life worth?

That's the question officials of the state of Maryland grappled with for several weeks before coming up with an answer recently — one that left Leslie Vass thinking: not enough.

For the record, Vass was sentenced to 20 years in jail back in 1975 after a delivery man fingered him as the kid who held him up outside a South Baltimore pharmacy.

At the time of his arrest, Vass was a gangling, 17-year-old high school basketball player whose only known offense off the basketball court was that he loitered on neighborhood corners after school — a largely innocent pastime of ghetto kids.

At his trial Vass kept telling people they had the wrong man, but nobody seemed to really listen. That's not so unusual.

"If you ask the people we put in jail, the prisons are all full of innocent people," a prosecutor said to me recently, not so tongue in cheek.

Vass was convicted and sentenced to 20 years in the human cesspool that is Maryland's prison system. Over the next 10 years he spent time in every major prison in the state, including one for mentally ill criminals.

But Vass never stopped proclaiming his innocence. He wrote to public officials, newspaper columnists, ministers and public defenders. It was with the latter that he hit pay dirt.

When an investigator for the state's public defender's office questioned the man whose testimony put Vass in prison, the man recanted.

"I had some doubt (at the trial). I wasn't sure. But there ain't no doubt in my mind now. I got the wrong man," he admitted.

Vass was released from prison in October 1984, slightly less than 10 years after his conviction. Two years later he received a full pardon for a crime his accuser now says Vass did not commit.

Last month Maryland officials grappled with the question: How much is 10 years of Leslie Vass's life worth?

How can the state compensate him for a decade of wrongful imprisonment? What price could be put on his lost opportunities, the shame and humiliation he and his family suffered — and the two stabbings he survived in prison?

There is no scientific formula for repairing such human damage. But to their credit, Maryland officials were of the mind to do something — to try in some way to let Vass know the state has a heart.

The three members of the Board of Public Works — the governor, the state treasurer and comptroller — labored over their decision. "How do you price an hour in prison?" Gov. William Donald Schaefer asked rhetorically at a public hearing.

"How do you help someone who hasn't had a bank account, who hasn't done his own shopping, who doesn't have the skills to operate on the outside?" the treasurer added.

Indeed, how do you put back together a life that the state has taken apart?

Vass's attorney said he had come up with the answer: one dollar for every minute of imprisonment. Maryland's debt to his client was the sum of $5.2 million, minus — of course — the attorney's princely fee.

State officials decided that Vass's lost years were worth $250,000 — $68 per day, not the $1,400 per day his attorney was seeking. The money is to be paid in monthly installments over the next six years, much like Maryland pays its big lottery winners.

The state also held out the prospect of a state job, and some non-financial help in enrolling in college and finding health insurance.

Vass, obviously disappointed with the decision, told a reporter, "I just want to walk away from here and get on with my life." Given what he has been forced to endure, there is probably no amount of money that can make Vass whole again, a reality that he probably has come to understand — not $250,000 nor $5.2 million.

We live in an imperfect society, one in which people, particularly minorities and the poor, are victimized daily because they are in the wrong place at the wrong time, or because of the color of their skin.

Vass is one of those victims, a man who has been scarred for life — a person who fell through the large cracks of our criminal justice system.

How much is 10 years of Leslie Vass's life worth? More than any of us can ever imagine.

Quiet riots

COLUMBIA, Md., March 7, 1988

The voices on the telephone answering machine were faint, but discernible.

Frederick Grimmel was mad as hell — upset when informed that Sherman Howell, a local activist, had telephoned earlier to question the minority-hiring practices of the country club Grimmel managed.

Returning the call, Grimmel reached only Howell's telephone answering machine and left a brief message. Then, thinking the recorder had shut off, he loosed the bigot inside him.

"This nigger, I am going to put him against the wall," he could be heard to say. "Sherman Nigger," he mocked. Nearby, someone else was heard to protest: "I'm discriminated against because all niggers get the jobs."

Within hours, Grimmel's recorded words — and the resulting public outcry — forced the club's owner to cut short his Florida vacation and rush home for damage control. At a hurriedly called news conference, Nicholas Mangione, a multimillionaire developer, apologized for his manager's remarks.

Saying "I have not had ample time to investigate," the Turf Valley Country Club owner added a personal note. "I have been called a wop and greaser, and I take it with a grain of salt."

Whatever point he was trying to make was lost on local officials of the NAACP and Chamber of Commerce, who called for Grimmel's dismissal.

Mangione's response? He suspended Grimmel, his nephew, with pay until he completes his investigation — an action one NAACP official termed "a paid vacation."

Twenty years after the Kerner Commission warned that "our nation is moving toward two societies, one black, one white — separate but unequal," events such as this seem to occur with alarming frequency.

Many of us know about Forsyth County, Ga., Howard Beach and The Citadel, where racial incidents spilled over into the national media spotlight. But unnoticed by far too many of us is the bigotry that festers largely out of public view.

And it is this kind of racial prejudice that is an underlying cause for the slow pace of progress made by blacks since 1968. Where once those who opposed integration and the political and economic advancement of blacks took to the streets to shout "nigger" in shrill defiance of civil rights protesters, most of today's racists are not so obvious.

Like Grimmel, they choose to vent their true feelings only in private. Unlike Grimmel, most of them have the good sense to hang up before letting go. Still, the damage they do is largely the same.

Earlier this month, a group of academicians, led by former Oklahoma senator and Kerner Commissioner member Fred Harris, issued an update on the Kerner report.

In contrast to the violence that gutted neighborhoods in many cities during the 1960s, "quiet riots" today are ravaging American cities, they concluded.

"These quiet riots are not as alarming or as noticeable to outsiders," members of Harris's panel wrote. "But they are even more destructive of human life than the violent riots of 20 years ago.

"Unemployment, poverty, social disorganization, segregation, family disintegration, housing and school deterioration, and crime are worse now" than during the 1960s when riots ravaged dozens of U.S. cities, panel members reported.

When the Kerner Commission report was issued in 1968, black unemployment was twice that of whites. Today, the percentage of blacks who are out of work is almost three times that of whites, the kind of troubling statistics that give rise to the concerns of activists about the hiring practices of employers such as Grimmel.

And there's more.

Housing in this country is still largely segregated. Even in the nation's capital, a city that is overwhelmingly black, a fair-housing group recent-

No justice, just us!

ly reported that blacks face a better than even chance of being discriminated against when trying to rent an apartment.

Also, most black children today attend schools that are overwhelmingly black, just as they did 20 years ago. This results not from legal discrimination, but from "white flight," a negrophobic reaction by whites to the dismantling of Jim Crow laws.

For a millionaire Italian-American developer and country club owner to be called a "wop" today may not be, for him, cause for concern.

But for a black to be called "nigger" by an employer simply because he inquires about fair employment practices ought to cause right-thinking people to shudder and — given what else we know about the condition of blacks — to wonder just how far we actually have come as a nation since 1968.

CHAPTER 3
A crying shame

THERE is much that happens these days that is capable of bringing a tear to my eyes.

Where once I prided myself on remaining dry-eyed and stoic in the face of some of life's most heart-wrenching tragedies, the increased frequency with which such events now occur has weakened my resolve and loosed my tear ducts.

The violent death of a mother at the hands of a brutal gang or the loss of a star basketball player to some killer cocaine are events whose hurt goes far beyond families and friends.

To look on as two sons of one of this nation's most revered civil rights activists go to jail — not in the name of social justice, but instead personal greed — is enough to wet the eyes of even a crusty old journalist.

Life is full of outrages. And where once I passed many of them off as the problems of others, I have now come to understand that human suffering creates a ripple effect that ultimately touches us all.

Now, when news of these trying times comes my way, I am inclined to experience an uncontrolled wetting of the eyes and to utter: "That's a crying shame." ■

A crying shame

Life on the tundra

WASHINGTON, Dec. 23, 1985

I cried the first time I read an account of what they did to Catherine Fuller.

She was a small woman whose life was marked by the ebb and flow of her existence on the edges of poverty in a big city ghetto.

The mother of six, she and her husband lived in a small house in a neighborhood littered with the signs of poverty and despair — dirty alleys, tattered buildings, and the ever-present milling groups of unemployed youths. It was with the latter that 48-year-old Catherine Fuller had a rendez-vous with destiny, and death.

On Oct. 1, 1984, she left the protection of her home, from which friends said she seldom ventured, to buy some medicine for a sore ankle. It was just before dusk.

Nearby, in a small park, a group of young men gathered in prey of a victim. They talked about robbing someone, or as they put it, "getting paid."

Catherine Fuller had less than $50 in her possession when the men forced her into an alley, one striking the side of her head with a two-by-four. She was stripped of her clothes, dragged across broken glass and beaten savagely.

As the 98-pound woman struggled with her attackers and pleaded for help, dozens of neighborhood people looked on. No one came to her assistance.

Then, in a final act of human violation, one of her assailants forced a pole 12 inches into Fuller's rectum. Later a medical examiner said she died from injuries similar to those sustained by victims in a high-speed car accident or a fall from a tall building.

Twelve young men — people with nicknames like "Snot Rag," "Hollywood" and "Fella" — and a teen-age girl were charged with the murder of Catherine Fuller.

As the 98-pound woman struggled with her attackers and pleaded for help, dozens of neighborhood people looked on. No one came to her assistance.

Fire at will

Two of the accused copped a plea and testified against the other defendants. One was granted a separate trial; the remaining were tried together.

Recently, a Washington jury convicted eight of the young men. Those found guilty of first-degree murder, armed robbery and kidnapping ranged in age from 17 to 21. Two defendants, including the lone female, were acquitted.

When I heard the verdict, I felt a rush of satisfaction. For months I had contemplated what measure of revenge "we" could visit upon "them." They were, I thought, deserving of no mercy.

The system had worked, but justice would only be served when these young men are called upon to forfeit their lives for the brutality they made Catherine Fuller suffer.

I remember reading what H.L. Mencken once said about the death penalty: "The only punishment worth anything at all," he said, "is the capital variety. It begs the question, but it at least gets rid of the concrete criminal . . . "

In my rage, I found myself agreeing with Mencken.

But few problems of any magnitude in this world are solved so easily.

The young men who so degraded and brutalized Catherine Fuller lived their lives out on the tundra of this society. They were not just unemployed, many were unemployable.

Their existence constitutes a kind of human cesspool from which they often prey upon decent people in this society. As much as anything else, they represent the failings of our system.

Maybe the easy way out for those of us who don't want to end up like Catherine Fuller is to, as Mencken suggests, beg the question and put these people — and all like them — to death. Maybe, but I'm not sure.

To accept such logic, I fear, is to give up a part of myself — that part that believes each of us shares some small measure of responsibility for the other's destiny.

The tundra on which people like the killers of Catherine Fuller exist is closer to most of us than we think. Yet, like the handicapped people whom we encounter on the streets, we often find them too disturbing to acknowledge.

Somehow we have got to find a way to grapple effectively with the problems of the poor and disenfranchised. While the traditional measures of the economic health of our nation suggest that life in America is improving for the vast majority of us, those who are on the fringes are close to inheriting a permanent legacy of poverty and despair.

Faced with this reality, some of them lose their self-respect, and their respect for human life and dignity. To ignore their plight is to condemn ourselves to a life haunted by their rage.

I grieve for Catherine Fuller, and I want those responsible for her death to pay society's price for their crime.

But I shudder to think how many other people are out there on the tundra who are about to snap. Somehow we have got to find a way to pull them into the American mainstream. Somehow we have got to find a way out of this vicious cycle of crime and punishment.

If not, we may all end up doing a lot of crying.

Pat's big cry

WASHINGTON, Oct. 4, 1987

Much has been made of the tears shed by Pat Schroeder when recently she exercised the good judgment to withdraw from next year's presidential sweepstakes.

A long shot for the Democratic Party nomination, in a race that is beginning to look more like a poorly staged re-enactment of George Armstrong Custer's last campaign, Schroeder had the good sense to break and run. That she cried in the process suggests we all have cause to mourn her political passing.

For far too long the body politic of this country has been stocked largely with men and women who are stripped of humility and compassion — except that which serves their political interests. Not so Pat Schroeder.

With the entire world looking on, she took to the political stump a few days ago to announce her resignation from the race for the Democratic Party's 1988 presidential nomination. "I couldn't figure out how to run and not be separated from those I serve," Schroeder said, choking back tears. "I could not bear to turn every human contact into a photo opportunity."

The media took to the moisture in her eyes like vultures to the stench of rotting flesh. The front pages of many newspapers carried emotionladened pictures of Schroeder fighting back her tears. *The Washington Post* ran a photo of her husband wiping the wetness from the Colorado congresswoman's eyes.

Not to be outdone, television networks put sound to this imagery and ran the story prominently on the evening news. USA TODAY asked a political consultant and Dr. Joyce Brothers about the tears Schroeder shed.

"Tears in politics at difficult moments are rarely a good thing," offered Mandy Grunwald, the political consultant.

"She had a real shot at the most important office in the land, and she ended up crying," Brothers said. "It is hard to visualize the president crying in front of Gorbachev."

Harder yet to believe is that a significant number of people would think Schroeder un-presidential for such a show of emotion in front of her friends and supporters.

A good friend of mine is always reminding me that "a person's true conviction comes from the heart, not from the head." It is a lesson that is lost on many politicians.

Pat Schroeder cried because she felt in her heart the frustration of trying to pull together a presidential campaign that does not lose contact with the people she was elected to serve. She was heartbroken by her decision to drop out of the Democratic Party race — a decision she knew would disappoint most of her followers.

That she did not render her decision to quit the race stoically suggests a level of personal compassion and humility that would be a refreshing addition to the Oval Office.

Just imagine how the course of history might have been changed if the men who have inhabited the White House had, on occasion, shed a few tears.

Maybe Lyndon Johnson would not have committed millions of U.S. servicemen to the mire of Vietnam if he had wept in the presence of the men who were advising him to send our soldiers to that conflict.

It is probable that Richard Nixon would have completed his second term of office if his eyes had teared up a bit when his aides told him of the Watergate break-in — and if he had reacted by reporting those responsible to the Washington police.

And if Ronald Reagan had cried a little during a Cabinet meeting for any of the hundreds of American servicemen who died as a result of his world adventurism in places like Grenada, Lebanon and the Persian Gulf, then maybe some of those lives could have been saved.

Humility and compassion ought to be as much a prerequisite for public office in this country as one's toughness and resolve.

If we have learned nothing else over the past quarter century it is that insulated, surly presidents, lacking the human compassion of a Pat Schroeder, have plunged this country into one national conflict after another.

I think the time has come for us to acknowledge compassion and humility as acceptable presidential character traits. No, I'm not suggesting that the world would be a better place if Reagan cries at his next summit meeting with Mikhail Gorbachev.

But what I am saying is that there is a lot of merit to that which my friend often says: "A person's true conviction comes from the heart, not from the head."

The candy man

WASHINGTON, July 5, 1986

Drug pushers and pimps are a curious lot. They are venal people who ply their trades with promises of erotic pleasures.

But what they actually deliver is short on pleasure and long on pain.

There is widespread contempt for the more obvious of these slime, most of whom mistakenly are thought to work their business in the shadows of our society — in the red-light districts and ghettos of America.

But because many an otherwise self-respecting citizen drinks at the fountain of their illusion, most drug pushers and pimps are able to sustain their business of human destruction despite the best efforts of this nation's constabulary.

Such a failing is a largely acknowledged, if not totally acceptable, predicament.

And so it is that those caught up in the tight grip of these vicious practices go mostly ignored — they are acceptable casualties in our national quest for pleasure and self-gratification. It is only when one of the victims has some measure of celebrity that the public groans its displeasure.

Fire at will

Such is the case of Len Bias, the star basketball player for the University of Maryland whose life came to an abrupt end late last month after he inhaled some unusually high-grade cocaine.

Bias' death came just a few hours after he was selected by the Boston Celtics in the first round of the National Basketball Association draft, an action that ensured him life-long financial security.

In death, he fell victim to both the drug pushers and the pimps of our society.

The former is the "candy man" who provided the collegiate star with the killer cocaine. A criminal investigation will run its course before the state of Maryland can fully assess blame and mete out a penalty for this homicidal act.

The latter — the pimps — are less obvious contributors to Bias's untimely demise.

Unlike the people who peddle sex for money, these pimps do not go about speaking of their work in hushed tones or cavorting around town in pink Cadillacs, with their stable of women at the ready.

The pimps who brought Len Bias to the point of his destruction are the men and women who manage college sports and run the nation's universities.

The playing fields of major college sports are human meat markets where the only real prerequisite for competition is an athlete's physical prowess — academic achievement be damned.

Many universities care little or nothing about educating these modern-day gladiators. College athletics is big business, with successful programs raking in millions of dollars annually.

In this environment, college recruiters, coaches and presidents are the pimps, and the athletes — a goodly number of whom get little education and never graduate — their prey.

The only lesson most of these kids learn is that more than a few school officials will set aside almost any rule for the sake of a winning athletic program.

Reports abound of recruiting violations and the large number of athletes who are talented enough to play intercollegiate sports for four years and help fatten their school's coffers, but not smart enough to earn a degree.

Len Bias's final semester at the University of Maryland was not spent in class. He failed three and withdrew from two of the five classes in which he enrolled.

Like their counterparts at many other universities, Maryland officials have shown scant concern for the fate of athletes who no longer are eligible to compete for the school.

Of course, none of this can be cited as directly causing Len Bias to take that fatal snort of cocaine. But the university is guilty of creating an environment in which promising young athletes are recruited and used — much like pimps use their whores — solely for the purpose of lining the school's pockets with money.

Little wonder that some of these young men also fall victim to the recruiting pitch of drug pushers with their little bags of "white candy."

A story worth telling

ATLANTIC CITY, N.J., Jan. 1, 1987

Celestine Tate is dying to meet Bill Cosby. She wants America's favorite television father to produce a movie version of her life story. Really!

And, if my opinion counts for anything, I think that the star of the nation's No. 1 television show ought to give her a call. Why? Because Tate's life story could be one of the most heart-wrenching movies to come out of Hollywood since *Imitation of Life.*

A quadriplegic, she was born with birth defects that left her arms and legs severely underdeveloped and useless. As a child growing up in Philadelphia, Tate regularly found herself on the painful end of tasteless jokes.

Eleven years ago, Tate gave birth to a daughter out of wedlock. Philadelphia's social service agency went to court in an effort to win custody of the infant, claiming that Tate could not possibly care for the child alone.

But the courageous black woman won the custody fight — and national media attention — after using her mouth to change the baby's diaper in the courtroom. "I can also cook and sew," said Tate, who at 31, now has two physically normal daughters.

"And I tie shoes with my mouth. I had to learn that. Who else was going to teach my children how it's done," she deadpanned.

Some story, huh, Bill? Well, there's more.

Fire at will

It was Tate's desire to provide for her children that caused her to learn to type with her tongue — that's right, her tongue.

"But nobody would give me a job," she complained. "They didn't think it would look very good for me to be handling paper with my mouth. People see me as being handicapped. My body is handicapped, but my mind is normal. And normal people want to work. I want to work."

Interested yet, Bill?

Next Tate went to Philadelphia's Settlement Music House and learned to play the electronic keyboard with her tongue. She began performing on local street corners and received small donations from passers-by.

Eventually, Tate took her one-woman show to the Atlantic City Boardwalk where, propped atop a gurney near Caesar's Hotel-Casino, she earned as much as $2,000 for a single day's performance. With the money she earns, Tate has hired a private nurse and driver.

But as in all good tear-jerkers there has got to be a villain, and this one is no exception.

Atlantic City officials cited Tate for violation of a 1910 law forbidding begging on its famed Boardwalk and saddled her with $2,000 in fines.

Tate, who said she used to go to public places with a cup looking for handouts, argued that she was performing for the contributions she received — not begging.

In an emotion-packed scene, more powerful than the courtroom drama in *Madame X,* Tate broke into an impromptu concert after the judge ordered her to pay the fines. Even the police who testified against her were moved to applause.

"I admire her greatly . . . her guts, her drive," the prosecutor confessed. "She's an inspiration. She's not one in a million. She's one in 218 million."

Defiantly, Tate said she would go to jail rather than pay the fines or stop performing on the Boardwalk. Her lawyer said he would challenge the constitutionality of the 76-year-old law.

Dry your eyes, Bill.

In November, Tate's lawyer and the prosecutor reached an out-of-court agreement that allows the gutsy woman to continue performing on the Boardwalk. For her part, Tate must apply for a city permit to

A crying shame

solicit, something she previously had been denied.

"I'm happy that they are not going to dispute it anymore," said Tate, who also is pursuing a degree in psychology at Temple University. "But I was going to continue anyway. I have my children to support."

Much of her sad story is already in book form, having been written by — you guessed it — Celestine Tate. "First I talked into a tape recorder, and then I typed the entire manuscript . . . all 149 pages," she said. "It's called *To Those Who Ask, Why Me?* I want Bill Cosby to produce it, but I don't know how to contact him."

So, come on, Bill. Give the lady a call.

Teetering on the brink

WASHINGTON, Sept. 4, 1988

Life on the edge has Lawrence Taylor teetering on the brink.

Taylor, in the opinion of many, is the best linebacker in professional football. A fierce competitor afield, he was to have been paid $1 million this year to maul opposition players.

In seven years of play with the New York Giants, Taylor has become what sportswriters like to call an "impact player" — a superstar in a profession where players are judged by their ability and willingness to use their bodies as battering rams.

L.T., as many call him, has few peers in this game.

He plays football with the intensity of Mike Tyson and the fluid motions of Wayne Gretzky. Where others seek to avoid the bone-crunching contact that could bring their careers to a quick end, Taylor seems to relish a head-on collision with a running back in much the same way that Evil Knievel covets a motorcycle jump across the Grand Canyon.

A few days ago, NFL officials announced that Taylor has been suspended from the game for a minimum of 30 days. His offense: He took one hit too many. Of cocaine, that is. It was the second time in less than a year that the Giants' superstar has fumbled a drug test.

The suspension may cost Taylor $250,000 in salary, the amount he would have earned for the four games he'll miss while participating in a mandatory drug rehabilitation program. While club officials now hint that their star linebacker may require more than 30 days to shake his drug habit, it is obvious they hope to get him back into uniform before too much of this year's football season slips away.

It seems football, and winning, are more important to club officials than getting the monkey off Taylor's back.

Taylor is a football player by training. He is a drug addict by habit. Last year he authored a book in which he talked about both football and drugs. It's titled *LT: Living On The Edge*.

As self-portraits go, Taylor's book wasn't very revealing except for the chapters he devoted to his earlier drug problems, those that came before July 1968, when the NFL adopted its current drug abuse program.

"I wasn't supposed to be doing it," Taylor said of his first encounter with cocaine, in 1982. "There was this and that campaign against it; every politician, police chief and Nancy Reagan were against it. But hell, with a guy like me, that almost made it more attractive."

And then he offered: "From very early on, the Giants knew who on the team was into drugs. They certainly knew I was because they let me know . . . If they wanted to bust me, fine. But I knew they weren't going to do that, not as long as I was who I was and my game was intact."

OK, so maybe team officials didn't know Taylor was using drugs back then. Maybe their star linebacker lied in his book when he said they turned their backs on his drug abuse. But they certainly know now — the whole world knows — that Taylor has a drug habit.

The question now is: What are they going to do about it?

Taylor is not going to beat his drug addiction unless he is able to reach deep down inside himself and muster the courage to fight this illness in much the same way he marshals the strength to blitz the quarterback late in a game.

Still, even with that, he will need the support and encouragement of the people who run the New York Giants and professional football.

Drug abuse in professional sports is probably no more widespread than in the rest of our society. But pro baseball, basketball, hockey and football attract the interest of millions of Americans.

Dealing forcefully, yet fairly, with drug addicts in these sports might send a badly needed message to others that this society has little tolerance for drug abusers. To get that message across will take a lot more than a 30-day suspension.

What Taylor needs is help — a real chance to kick his ugly habit.

What he doesn't need is a gentle slap on the wrist and a quick return to uniform.

"If I were Joe Blow, OK, there'd be the slammer or some midnight trip to Betty Ford's farm . . . It was almost a thrill in itself knowing that people knew what I was doing and wouldn't do a damn thing to stop me," Taylor wrote in his book.

Somebody needs to do something to stop Lawrence Taylor before he self-destructs — someone who cares a lot more about getting him back on his feet than returning him to the playing fields of the NFL.

Tarnished image

BALTIMORE, June 4, 1988

It was a sad sight.

The two men stood ramrod straight on the steps of the federal courthouse and glared defiantly into television cameras and the eyes of waiting reporters.

And even now, only moments after having been sentenced to prison terms, they continued to plead their case — telling all who would listen that they are innocent victims of a government campaign to get black politicians.

For brothers Michael and Clarence Mitchell the end of an era was at hand. The time had come for these members of one of the nation's most prominent civil rights families to accept their fate. On April 5, they will begin serving the 30-month sentence a judge gave the brothers after a jury found them guilty of obstructing a federal investigation and wire fraud.

When they exchange their stylish suits for prison garb, the Mitchell brothers will bring to an end two promising political careers. They will also strip their family name of some of its luster and a reputation for honesty and integrity that was nurtured over the last 50 years.

Michael, 42, and Clarence, 48, are the sons of Clarence Mitchell Jr., the former Washington lobbyist for the NAACP — a man so influential with members of Congress that he came to be called the "101st senator." They are also the children of Juanita Jackson Mitchell, the feisty civil rights lawyer and activist whose mother is an NAACP legend. Parren Mitchell, their uncle, was Maryland's first black member of Congress.

There was a time when people in this city saw no limit to what the Mitchell brothers could accomplish. Clarence was for many years a state senator and Michael served on the Baltimore City Council. Michael was elected to fill his brother's senate seat in 1986, the year Clarence ran unsuccessfully to replace his retiring uncle in Congress.

As the political aspirations of blacks in this city grew over the years, the names of Michael and Clarence Mitchell were mentioned as potential beneficiaries of the burgeoning black vote.

They were also well known to Democratic Party presidential candidates, like Hubert Humphrey, Jimmy Carter and Walter Mondale who journeyed to Baltimore in search of the Mitchell brothers' support and that of other members of their politically powerful family.

But in recent years things started to change.

People began to whisper about allegations of wrongdoing. There were reports of financial problems and accusations of unethical activities. Some blacks who once voted Clarence and Michael into political office now called them "sleazy."

As their legal problems began to surface, the Mitchell brothers tried to turn their case into a civil rights cause — arguing that federal officials were out to get them for their many years of work "in the struggle."

But few people came to the rallies they called in Baltimore and Washington. One man told me: "I'll listen more closely to what they have to say about being picked on when they start to make a serious effort to answer the charges against them."

And in the end that's what it came down to, answering the charges brought against them by federal prosecutors.

The government charged that Clarence and Michael Mitchell accepted $50,000 from officials of the Wedtech Corporation, a New York defense contractor, in return for agreeing to try to block an investigation of the firm by a congressional committee headed by Parren Mitchell. Their uncle was not implicated in the scheme.

Ironically, Attorney General Edwin Meese, whose Justice Department prosecutors brought the Mitchells to trial, is himself thought to be a target in the ongoing criminal investigation of Wedtech.

At the sentencing hearing, everyone seemed to agree that the real victim in this case is the Mitchell family's good name. The prosecutor accused the brothers of betraying the family's "legacy of public achievement." The defense cited the family's contributions to the civil rights movement. The judge told the two men they had let greed sully their family's good name and reputation.

As Michael and Clarence Mitchell later stood on the federal courthouse steps, vowing that they would win their case on appeal, word spread of yet another charge of misdeeds.

Earlier in the day a city grand jury indicted Michael Mitchell, a practicing attorney, on charges of stealing the life insurance benefits of the 3-year-old son of a murder victim who was his client.

And in what will be the cruelest of ironies, he will soon stand trial on these charges in the municipal courthouse that bears his father's name. A sadder sight I can't imagine.

An ungodly act

CHARLOTTE, N.C., April 25, 1988

There is apparently no end to the crimes people will commit in the name of religion.

History books are full of reports of the carnage that has been wrought in the name of the Almighty. From the great Crusades of the 13th century to the apartheid of 20th century South Africa, men and women of the cloth have given license to some of our worst moral failings.

It was in the churches of the American South that plantation owners prayed on Sundays for good crops and healthy "niggras" to work their fields. Today, Protestants and Catholics in Northern Ireland butcher each other daily for the right to dominate that country's secular affairs. And in the Middle East, Jews and Moslems are locked into a vicious cycle of brutality over control of a small patch of earth they each call the Holy Land.

More than an opiate of the masses, religion has become for far too many an excuse for their ungodly acts, or the reason why such transgressions should simply be overlooked.

Earlier this month members of the Christian Ministers Fellowship Association, an interdenominational group of ministers, called upon Charlotte-area voters to re-elect County Commissioner Bob Walton.

A five-term incumbent, Walton is a Presbyterian minister who last year was convicted of sexually assaulting an 18-year-old high school student in his church. The homosexual encounter drew Walton a 30-day jail sentence and caused him the loss of his pulpit.

Now, less than three months after his release from jail, Walton is running for re-election to the Mecklenburg County Board of Commissioners in a campaign in which religion is a major issue. His principal opponent in the May 3 Democratic primary is Nasif Majeed, a local businessman whose Islamic faith is drawing more questions than Walton's criminal record.

And while local religious leaders have sought to exact a pledge from Majeed not to raise Walton's sexual assault conviction during this campaign, they have been quick to take the Moslem candidate to task for his religious beliefs.

"We've got a Christian who is running, one who espouses Christianity," the president of the Christian Ministers Fellowship Association said in announcing the group's endorsement of Walton.

As for Majeed, who has used code words like "morality" and "integrity" to focus attention on Walton's conviction, he argues that voters deserve a better role model.

"I believe in leadership by example," Majeed, a Burger King franchise operator, said shortly before the primary. "I think we have a responsibility to be good role models to our youth." It was a statement that drew the rancor of the ministers supporting Walton.

"We look for role models in the home," one minister responded. "If my daughter wants a role model, she looks to her mother and not someone in Congress."

Maybe so, but doesn't she deserve more role models than the home can produce?

What kind of statement do voters make when they choose a Christian of any ilk over a non-Christian candidate, simply on the basis of religion?

Sure, Bob Walton shouldn't be punished the rest of his life for the sexual assault he committed. And yes, he has paid the price for his crime. But I think Majeed is on to something when he talks about role models.

I, for one, am fed up with elected officials who violate their public trust. I'm tired of reading about congressmen who get swept up in sting operations. I'm made angry by officeholders who sell their services to the highest bidder and those who put personal gain before public service.

Being a public official is a thankless job. They live their lives in a fishbowl, surrounded on all sides by people who question their every move.

And in many ways having a public office is much like being a member of the clergy. People tend to hold you to a higher standard — to expect more of you than they do of themselves.

What we need in this world, I am certain, are a lot more role models. What we can do without are ministers who think otherwise.

A cheap shot

BALTIMORE, Sept. 14, 1988

"Are you voting against the gun ban?" the caller wanted to know.

It was early evening and my wife and I had just finished our dinner when the telephone rang. The voice on the other end was that of a telephone canvasser — a black woman who said she was calling from the Maryland Committee Against the Gun Ban.

"I said, are you voting against the gun ban," she repeated as I struggled to pull together the right words to answer her.

The call was the latest volley to be fired in the fight that is being waged — most hotly in Baltimore's black community — to reverse a Maryland gun control law that is said to be the nation's strictest.

The law, which was enacted earlier this year, allows a state appointed board to determine the kind of handgun that can be manufactured and sold in Maryland. Opponents of the law, led by the National Rifle Association, have petitioned it to referendum in November.

And with just a few weeks to go before the Nov. 8 vote, supporters and opponents of the law are waging the kind of shootout that makes what happened at the O.K. Corral look like a fireworks display.

In Baltimore's black community, cheap handguns — the kind the Maryland law is designed to prohibit — are the badge of courage of teen-age thugs who have made murder the leading cause of death for young black men.

The woman who called me probably didn't think much about the human carnage these cheap handguns have produced. It's not likely she has much of an emotional investment in the issue she's raising. And that's too bad.

She is probably more concerned about earning the $6.10 an hour gun-ban opponents are paying people to telephone city voters. Unemployment among Baltimore blacks takes an even greater toll here than do the deadly Saturday night specials.

But as I labored to find the words to answer her question, I thought of the many nameless casualties of the urban war being waged in inner cities across this nation — communities that are ravaged by the drug trade, and the crimes that spin off from this illicit activity.

I remember the trembling voice of a friend who once called me after finding out that his 11-year-old son had taken a handgun to school.

"He told me he just wanted to stop some boys from picking on him," my friend said in explanation of his son's action. "I'm just damn glad he didn't take it out of his locker." So was I.

The National Rifle Association argues that "guns don't kill, people do." Sure, but if you ever find yourself staring down the barrel of one of those cheap handguns — the kind that are now so easy to get in most big cities — try finding some comfort in that thought.

The call I received from the Maryland Committee Against the Gun Ban was one of thousands being made to get Baltimore blacks to vote in support of the referendum to kill the state's gun law.

Ironically, much of this effort is being managed by a black-owned, Washington-based public relations firm that is trying to convince black voters that banning cheap handguns will make it harder for them to defend their homes and property.

It's an argument members of Baltimore's Interdenominational Ministerial Alliance don't buy.

The 150 pastors who make up the alliance are banking on the influence they have with black voters to help beat back the attempt to void the Maryland law, which is not scheduled to take effect until 1990.

"How will you vote, sir?" the caller persisted when I asked her to repeat the question. "Will you be voting against the gun ban?"

No, I answered softly.

I wanted to say more, but the caller quickly hung up. I wanted to ask her if she lived in the inner city. If she had children. I wanted to know if she owned a Saturday night special. Or if she cared that others in her neighborhood might.

But her call was unexpected and her questions came so quickly, it was all I could do to utter the single word.

I wanted to say more, but now I'll just have to wait until Election Day to let my vote speak for me.

Foul play

WASHINGTON, April 16, 1989

Here in the nation's capital, where a politician's bluster fouls the air faster than a barnyard full of manure, it is impossible these days to escape the stench.

Much of the offending odor seems to be the product of two men who run the risk of becoming bigger public polluters than the Exxon Corporation.

When William Bennett announced this week his plan to use $80 million and a platoon of federal law enforcement officers to combat the illegal drug trade in Washington, the air quality index in this town fell sharply.

Blaming city officials for letting drug-related violence get out of control, Bennett says he will enlist the help of the FBI, civilian and military intelligence officers and federal lawyers to arrest and convict rampaging junkies and their pushers.

Imagine. Platoons of U.S. bureaucrats — maybe even some veterans of the federal government's failed effort to stop illegal drugs from entering this country — will take to the streets of Washington's ghettos to help local officials turn the tide of battle in a drug war that has claimed 135 lives already this year.

Can it be long before we'll see these G-men on television's evening news hauling drug dealers off to jail? How long will it be before Bennett stands in front of a gaggle of reporters to claim victory in this, his first major encounter with the bad guys of the drug trade?

Bennett's assault on Washington's drug problem amounts to little more than a "photo opportunity" for the overmatched drug czar, and a headline-grabbing news story for members of the capital's bloated press corps.

Fire at will

The $80 million he has committed to this skirmish is far short of the assistance sought by Mayor Marion Barry, Washington's other major source of air pollution. Barry asked federal officials for $102 million last week to hire 700 additional police, more judges and probation officers.

Sadly, the mayor's call for help came only after members of Congress — who still hold significant sway over city government operations — began to publicly take him to the woodshed for failing to reduce the level of drug-related violence in Washington.

Wounded politically by an endless string of negative press reports — stories about his suspected drug use and investigations into reports of fraud and abuse within his government — Barry has begun to suggest privately that he is the victim of racism.

And while there are bigots in the ranks of those who are out to get Barry, the black mayor has no one to blame for his current problems but himself. Bad judgment — and questionable advisers — have become a cornerstone of his administration. Last week, for example, Barry named Mary Treadwell, his ex-wife, to a task force to help clean up his, and the city's, tattered image. Treadwell, a convicted felon, did time for ripping off money from a government-funded anti-poverty program.

For his part, Bennett is guilty of staging a media campaign against drug traffickers, rather than an all-out assault upon those who have turned the United States into the world's most drug-dependent society.

Even if Bennett is successful in rooting drug dealers out of the nation's capital, officials in Maryland and Virginia fear he will only send the thugs scurrying into their jurisdictions.

And what about New York, Detroit, Miami and Los Angeles? What will be the solution to their growing drug problems? More money and federal agents?

Given the long-term poverty we see in urban ghettos — and the big profits people who live in them earn from the drug trade — it'll take more than police action to win the drug war we have chosen to fight on U.S. streets, rather than in the coca-growing fields of South America.

And for anyone to suggest otherwise only contributes further to the political pollution that fouls the air of our nation's capital.

A dream deferred

WASHINGTON, March 6, 1986

Nothing anguishes me more than to watch someone self-destruct.

Last week I looked on as Michael Ray Richardson's world exploded. A star guard on the New Jersey Nets basketball team, he succumbed to his drug addiction, in the process forfeiting much of a four-year, $3 million contract and a life of luxury that most of us can only dream about.

For the third time since 1983, Richardson has "fouled out" of the National Basketball Association on cocaine.

This time he drew a permanent ban from the sport that has been in his blood for a majority of his 30 years — long before cocaine was introduced into his system. He can appeal the banning order after two years.

As a youngster growing up in a South Baltimore ghetto, I idolized athletes. They were my role models. I remember sitting glued to the television set in the winters of my youth watching Johnny Unitas and Lenny Moore lead the Baltimore Colts to victory.

Each year when baseball's spring training got under way, I would rush home to read daily newspaper accounts from the Orioles' camp.

There was the time that shortstop Willie Miranda, who was always a late arrival, rode into spring training early on the back of a donkey.

And I remember the spring trainings that introduced me to "Diamond Jim" Gentile, Jim Palmer and Frank Robinson.

During those early years, professional basketball, too, was a major part of my life.

The now-Washington Bullets were then the Baltimore Bullets, and I regularly sat riveted to my radio to hear the exploits of Earl "The Pearl" Monroe, Gus Johnson and Jack Marin as they fought their classic battles with the likes of Bill Bradley, Walt Frazier and Willis Reed, of the New York Knicks. I was a consummate sports fan.

Sports offered me a kind of hope for the future that was unmatched in the classrooms of the public schools I attended. Sports stars were held out to me as alternative role models to the pimps, drug pushers and third-rate criminals who inhabited the neighborhood in which I lived. I dreamed of playing professional sports — baseball, basketball or football — and escaping to a better life.

Even as an adult, I continued to fantasize about being a star athlete, of being the idol and role model for millions of youngsters.

Fire at will

Professional sports are, for me, a dream deferred.

But in the last couple of years, my dream world has begun to crumble. Piece by piece it's come apart as many athletes I admired turned out to be more adept at consuming illegal drugs than at hitting a curve, running off tackle or making a three-point basket.

In fact, so many professional athletes have been linked to cocaine recently that new meaning is given to the phrase "Coke is it."

Between 1980 and 1985, 18 professional athletes were suspended for their involvement with illegal drugs. Last week, just a couple days after Richardson's banning, baseball Commissioner Peter Ueberroth conditionally suspended 21 players for their alleged use of cocaine.

It's true that professional sports leagues have attempted to control drug abuse among players through various educational and treatment programs. But, alas, for me, and many others, it's too late.

The innocence is gone.

When a ball is dropped, a basket missed or a play blown, I wonder if the players are high. It's unfair, I know, to think like that, but I do. With each new report of a drug-abusing athlete, my image of those who play professional sports is ruptured more.

Nearly forty years ago, Langston Hughes wrote *Dream Deferred,* a poem about dashed hopes and ruptured images:

> "What happens to a dream deferred?
> Does it dry up
> like a raisin in the sun?
> Or fester like a sore —
> and then run?
> Does it stink like rotten meat?
> Or crust and sugar over —
> like a syrupy sweet?
> Maybe it just sags
> like a heavy load.
> Or does it explode?"

Last week Michael Ray Richardson's basketball career came to an abrupt end. Having gone one-on-one with cocaine, he was called for a technical foul and thrown out of the game.

And what happened to my dream deferred?

It exploded.

CHAPTER 4
Ungawah Jones

THERE is a bit of Ungawah Jones in every black American. He is that side of us that cringes at the first sight and sound of racial insensitivity. He surfaces quickly — though not always noticeably — every time we go house hunting, job hunting or have our car stopped late at night by a police officer.

Ungawah Jones is the black radical in all of us — a voice deep within that is ever doubting of the progress we've made and the obstacles we've overcome. He is the troubling conscience of middle-class blacks, who are often made to feel guilty about our measured progress and the charge by some white conservatives that *we* have abandoned those blacks who seem trapped in America's underclass.

As a young boy growing up in a South Baltimore housing project, my Saturday mornings were devoted to watching reruns of programs that reinforced white America's sense of self: *Our Gang*, *The Bowery Boys* and a seemingly endless chain of Tarzan movies. It was from the latter that Ungawah Jones sprang.

Tarzan was "King of the Jungle." A lone white man whose very presence sent unfriendly African tribesmen racing in retreat. And simply by yelling out the word "umgawa," he could summon help from friendly tribes or menacing animals. A word of universal applications that was created by writers at MGM, "umgawa" allowed Tarzan to dominate all of black Africa by uttering this meaningless sound.

Ungawah Jones will brook no such domination of himself or his people. His is a persistent voice of protest. An ever-present challenge to those whose words and deeds deny blacks entry into the American mainstream.

More than my alter ego, he is the consciousness within that won't let me rest until our deferred dreams become reality. ■

Yo, Shakespeare

LOS ANGELES, May 23, 1988

"Yo, Shakespeare," the dashiki-wearing man called out to me from across the hotel lobby. "You here to cover the presidential campaign?"

No, I snapped, angered by my longtime friend's annoying habit of mockingly comparing my newspaper columns to the works of the English playwright.

What are you doing in California? I asked him. What are you protesting this time?

"Hey, like I'm always 'bout something serious, man," he responded. "I don't waste my time doodling 'gar-bage' for the white man."

For Ungawah Jones — a 1960s radical and figment of my imagination — most things in life are reduced to a consideration of black and white.

"I'm here to get into the race, brother. I'm gonna take my act all the way to the White House."

What are you talking about, Ungawah? I asked.

"I'm running for president, man. Come November, I'm gonna be your new leader," he said.

Wait a minute, Ungawah, I answered. Isn't it a little late for you to be getting into the campaign? Everybody knows that George Bush and Michael Dukakis are going to be their party's nominees.

"Yeah, and I'm gonna be my party's nominee," Ungawah shot back. "I'm doin' what Jesse should have done. I started my own party. I'm the candidate of the Afro-American People's Party.

"You see, Jesse messed up. He let 'em con him into joinin' their team — they told him he could be a player in their party, and now he's 'bout to be benched, permanently."

Come on, Ungawah, what are you talking about? Jesse Jackson has been a major player in this year's presidential campaign.

"I don't waste my time doodling 'gar-bage' for the white man. . . . I know what it takes to make things right in this country. I'm gonna name Stokeley Carmichael secretary of state and H. Rap Brown defense secretary."

"See, that's where you don't know what you're talkin' 'bout, fool. The primaries ain't nothin' but spring training. The real season doesn't start until the general election campaign begins in September, and by then, Jesse will be on the sidelines," Ungawah explained.

"That's them smart-ass white boys that Andy Young was talkin' 'bout. They saw how popular Jesse has become and tricked him right out of the real race.

"Now it's up to me to be the first black man in the White House."

But how can you get the votes? I asked. You don't have any experience in elected office.

"That's the propaganda they ran down on Jesse. Hey, man, I'm gonna do it the same way Ronald Reagan did," Ungawah said.

"I got this Haitian brother on my campaign staff. He can work some serious roots on folks. He's got some stuff brewin' for them racists in South Africa that I'm savin' for Inauguration Day.

"I even broke down and hired a college-educated sister to be my press secretary. Her name is Janet Cooke. She used to work for that liberal rag *Washington Post*."

Hold on, Ungawah. Janet Cooke lost her job at the *Post* after she got caught making up quotes.

"Yeah, well, that was a bad move on the *Post's* part. She made the paper look good — won it a Pulitzer Prize," he countered.

"Janet Cooke can do for me what Larry Speakes did for Reagan. Make me look good. A president needs a press secretary who has a way with words."

I don't know, Ungawah. It all sounds a little crazy to me. Nobody wants to see a black president in the White House more than I do, but I don't think America is ready for you.

"Well, ready or not, here I come. I'm in this race to stay. I know what it takes to make things right in this country. I'm gonna name Stokeley Carmichael secretary of state and H. Rap Brown defense secretary.

"And to prove I'm not a black racist, I'm gonna make my man William Kunstler attorney general," Ungawah offered proudly.

It seems that you have things figured out, I conceded. All you need to do now is win in November.

"No problem. You know the Haitian brother I was tellin' you about, the one who works the roots? Well, he's figured out how I can wipe out America's trade deficit, balance the budget, and fund a war of liberation in South Africa without raisin' taxes.

"What do you call that if it's not a winnin' strategy?" Ungawah asked.

How about voodoo economics? I answered.

Presidential debate

WASHINGTON, Sept. 21, 1988

"Wake up, geek. I need your help."

It was 3 a.m. and the voice on the other end of the telephone was full of emotion.

"Hey, man. This is important," the caller yelled into the phone, his words striking against my ear with the force of a well-placed jab.

Ungawah, is that you, Ungawah, I whispered into the mouthpiece of my phone.

"Damn right it's me, man. Now wake up, 'cause we've got a problem."

What do you mean, "we've got a problem?" I shot back at Ungawah Jones.

"Like I said, man. We've got a problem. You still black, right?"

Yeah, Ungawah, I answered slowly. I'm still black.

"Well then, if you're black, you got to help me."

Help you how, Ungawah? I asked. It's 3 o'clock in the morning.

"I'm at the bus station, man. On my way to North Carolina for the debate. You know, the one between Bush and Dukakis. You got to let me borrow your press pass," he said.

What for, I asked, more than a bit fearful of his answer.

"Cause I want to ask these chumps some serious questions, man, 'bout what they gonna do for black folks," Ungawah responded.

Are you crazy, Ungawah? You show up in Winston-Salem with my press pass trying to get into the debate and your butt's going to land in jail, I said.

"You let me worry 'bout that," Ungawah snapped back. "Just let me have your press pass so I can get goin'.'"

Hold it, Ungawah. I'm not letting you use my press pass. Besides, it wouldn't do you any good. Only the three journalists selected by the

Dukakis and Bush campaigns will get to ask the candidates any questions.

"Say what! You mean these guys decide who gets to ask the questions? This thing is worse than I thought," he said.

Look, Ungawah, I've got to get some sleep. Call me back in the morning, I said.

"Don't you hang up on me, geek. I want that press pass," he shouted. "I'm gonna get into that debate and I'm gonna ask my questions, if it's the last thing I ever do."

It will be, Ungawah, if you disrupt a televised presidential debate.

"Look, man, I'm not anxious to end up in the joint, but somebody's got to force these guys to deal with black folks' issues," Ungawah said.

Listen, I implored him. The journalists who'll question Bush and Dukakis will probably raise a broad range of issues. Subjects like the environment, the federal deficit and national defense. There ought to be something there for everybody in this country.

"Hey, man. Black folks have heard enough talk 'bout those issues. It's time Bush and Dukakis start talkin' 'bout something else," Ungawah responded.

Like what? I asked.

"Like, what's gonna be their Southern Africa policy? Like, what are they gonna do to reduce black unemployment; to keep drugs out of the black community? What are they gonna do to feed hungry black children and reduce the black infant mortality rate? Like . . ."

All right, man. All right. I conceded. I get your point.

"Yeah, well I'm not sure you do," he shot back. "These guys have been all over the country campaignin' and just about the only time they mention anything 'bout blacks they are standin' in the middle of Harlem or Watts.

"You see, it's easy for them to say they're concerned 'bout us when they're surrounded by a few hundred black folks. Hell, even Ronald Reagan will do that.

"But I want to hear them tell the rest of America that they intend to do something 'bout the problems of black folks," Ungawah said. "I want to know just how much commitment these guys really have to us."

Well, my friend, I said. I just hope you know what you're doing. But whatever you do, you'll have to do it without my press pass.

"Hey man, forget your press pass," Ungawah said. "I don't have to attend a presidential debate to get my point across. You get some sleep. I'll meet you at 9 a.m. — in your office."

In my office, for what? I asked.

"The two of us are gonna write your next column," he responded.

Boycotting Japan

WASHINGTON, Sept. 30, 1987

For Ungawah Jones, the clock stopped running sometime during the height of the 1960s' civil rights movement.

He was then, and is now, a devout black revolutionary. He still goes about dressed in a dashiki, quoting Malcolm X and Marcus Garvey. He brandishes his sense of outrage over the condition of blacks like a badge of courage earned on America's civil rights battlefields.

As much a figment of my imagination as a living breathing soul, he is a friend of long-standing. Last week he reappeared in my life.

"Yo, DeWayne, what's happenin'," Ungawah shouted, rushing to my side as I walked one of the capital's busiest streets.

Hey, Ungawah, I answered. How are things with you?

"On my way to a rally," he said. "We gonna throw down on that dude Nakasone. Gonna make him sorry he ever dumped on black folks."

What are you talking about, Ungawah? I asked.

"Yo, brother, we gonna take him to the wall. We 'bout tired of these foreigners puttin' the bad mouth on black folks," Ungawah responded, the swagger in his walk now becoming even more pronounced.

"Remember back in 1980 when that Israeli general, the one who wore the patch on one eye, put us down? Said there were nothin' but a lot of dumb blacks in the army.

"And then, in 1982, them ungrateful Europeans started sneakin' around talkin' 'bout there were too many black soldiers overseas. They even asked the Pentagon to bring some of the brothers home, man," Ungawah complained.

"We let them off the hook, but we're not gonna chill out on Nakasone. Man, not only did he call all black Americans dumb, but he threw in the Puerto Ricans and Mexicans too. We gonna organize a boycott of Japanese products — gonna hit them where it hurts, in the wallet."

Wait a minute, Ungawah, I interrupted. The Japanese government offered an explanation to the State Department.

"Say what? An explanation to the State Department. How many blacks, Puerto Ricans and Mexicans do they have over there?" he countered.

And, Ungawah, I continued, the Japanese ambassador also read the prime minister's apology to members of the Congressional Black Caucus. Doesn't that put things right? I asked.

"Hey, if the folks in the caucus are willin' to settle for that jive apology," Ungawah said, "then maybe Nakasone was right — at least 'bout a few of us.

"Look, we've got an opportunity to mobilize, like in the old days. This guy Nakasone can be the new George Wallace. Remember in the '60s, when old George, Lester Maddox and Bull Connor used to make black folks so mad?

"Well now we can use what Nakasone said to rally us together again — this time to get more economic equality," Ungawah said. "This is our chance to practice some of that self-help that conservatives are always talkin' 'bout.

"So let's organize a boycott of Japanese products. Get our friends in the unions to refuse to unload Japanese cargoes. Hell, man, we could even have sit-ins at some sushi bars," he added.

I don't understand, Ungawah, I said. The man's already apologized. What's the point?

"See, that's why you should never have left the movement, 'cause you don't think straight anymore," Ungawah shot back. "Now if he is really apologetic, let him show some sincerity and give us a few Toyota dealerships.

"And how about a couple of Sony distributorships? Hey, if his remorse is really heartfelt, it shouldn't be too much to expect some interest-free loans to help a few black folks get into business. Maybe the exclusive North American marketing rights to Hitachi or Panasonic? How about that for starters?" Ungawah asked with a big smile.

It sounds to me like you're trying to pick Japan's pockets, I said.

"Are you kidding, man? Do you know how deep in debt America is to Japan?" Ungawah asked. "About one-third of our foreign debt is owed to these dudes. Ask some U.S. auto or steel workers if they care. Hey, here's a chance for blacks to get outta the economic hole and bring some jobs back to this country at the same time. And that's the kind of affirmative action that won't turn off too many white folks."

Well, I muttered, I don't know, Ungawah.

"Look, I see I'm wastin' my time with you," Ungawah said, sounding more than a bit annoyed. "I've got to get to the rally.

"By the time we finish with Nakasone, we're gonna clear up this country's balance of payments and put a lot of black folks on easy street.

"Sayonara, baby."

Battle ready

NEW ORLEANS, Aug. 19, 1988

There he was, dressed in camouflage fatigues, standing in the shadow of "Big Daddy's Topless Bar," in the middle of one of Bourbon Street's bawdy blocks.

Ungawah, Ungawah Jones. What are you doing here, dressed like that? I called out to my longtime friend.

"Hey, brother. Can't be too careful. They're all over the place," he answered.

Who? Ungawah. All over where?

"Them damn conservatives, man. They're thicker than thieves 'round here. Got to be on my guard, brother. Got to be ready to throw down with them dudes," he said.

Give me a break, Ungawah. I'm here to cover the Republican National Convention. I don't have time for your war games, man.

"Well you better make some time," Ungawah snapped. "'Cause if them conservatives take over this country black folks are gonna be history."

Ungawah, this is 1988. Ronald Reagan is president and the conservatives are already in control of the government, I said, annoyed that this obvious fact had escaped his notice.

"Not the Reagan conservatives, brother. They're bad enough. But that's not the bunch I'm talkin' 'bout," he said.

"See, that's the problem. It's hard for a lot of folks to distinguish them. I'm tellin' you, man, there is a group of those conservatives who are real extremists — you know, a kind of Christian, Islamic Jihad. And they're determined to finish off black folks."

Yeah, well I don't see it, Ungawah. A conservative is a conservative. They're all the same, I said.

"Damn, man. Did you see the movie *Predator?* Remember how that creature from outer space was able to make himself look like a tree? Remember how he blended in with the jungle?

"Well, that's what these dudes do. They blend in with all the other conservatives, but they are a much more deadly breed," Ungawah warned.

Now I see, Ungawah. Arnold Schwarzenegger is our enemy, I said with a big grin.

"Listen, geek. I don't have time to play with you. People like Reagan and Bush are decoys. They are just trees in the jungle compared to the guys I'm talkin' 'bout. The predator is that guy Gordon Humphrey," Ungawah said, referring to the ultraconservative Republican senator from New Hampshire. "He's the real Great Satan."

Hey, Ungawah. I can see the light on in your head, but I don't think anybody's home up there. What the heck are you talking about?

"This guy Humphrey is out to trash us, I'm tellin' you. And he's not alone," said Ungawah, his eyes sweeping the crowded streets for signs of "the enemy."

Is that right? I asked in a condescending voice.

"I ain't jivin', man. He's the one who pressured Bush into puttin' that Quayle guy on his ticket."

You mean Indiana Sen. Dan Quayle? I asked. Bush's vice presidential running mate?

"Right. He's a Humphrey clone. They're both anti-civil rights and anti-affirmative action," Ungawah said. "If these guys had their way, Robert Bork would be the next attorney general."

Even if this is true, Ungawah, I don't see how one man, or two, can be a great threat to 25 million blacks, I challenged him.

"Hey, they're not alone. It's Humphrey and Quayle. And it's also New Hampshire Gov. John Sununu and Jerry Falwell — the Moral Majority head mullah — and a lot more," he explained.

"Hell, I saw Cal Thomas, that ultraconservative columnist, out here on Bourbon Street the other day," Ungawah whispered. "I'm tellin' you man, they're all over the place."

OK, Ungawah, I conceded. We're surrounded by hostile conservatives. So what do we do?

"Now you're talkin' brother. We've got to organize. Get the word out. We can't let them predators pick us off one by one," my radical friend cautioned. "If this guy Quayle gets anywhere near the White House, we may all end up on a fast train ride to nowhere, if you know what I mean."

I understand Ungawah, but . . .

"No buts, geek. This is war," he said angrily. "And we're only gonna get one shot at these guys this year."

When? I asked.

"Early in November. And we've got to be ready," he answered. "You are registered to vote . . . right?"

Lone picket

BALTIMORE, April 13, 1987

The lone picket outside of Memorial Stadium walked with the snap of a veteran protester. His placard, thrust high into the air, carried an angry message: "Baseball's Executive Suite Off-Limits To Blacks."

Clinging to the sign was a man whose flowing dashiki and unmistakable glare were all too familiar.

It was Ungawah Jones, my old friend.

Man, what are you doing here? I asked.

"Raisin' hell, brother," he shot back. "Somebody's got to let folks know how racist the people who run baseball are. Did you hear that dude Al Campanis on *Nightline?* Said blacks are too dumb to be baseball executives."

Yeah, Ungawah, I saw it. The program about the Los Angeles Dodgers' executive got me so upset I decided to write a column.

"Oh yeah, when?" Ungawah demanded, breaking stride to confront me. "When you gonna do that, after tonight's ballgame? Gonna go in and give the Orioles your money first, chump?"

As I started to answer, Ungawah pushed his placard against my chest. "Here, take this. I got another one. We can walk together — that is if that ol' soft newspaper job of yours hasn't made you forget that you're still black."

Well . . . yeah, I was going to the game. But you've got a good point. Why should I give them my money, I asked rhetorically, as I fell in step beside Ungawah.

"So what you gonna say, man?" he asked. "What you gonna say in your column 'bout these baseball bigots?"

Well, I'm going to point out that of the 26 major league teams, only 11 employ any minorities in management positions. That only 30 of the 879 top administrative jobs in baseball are held by minorities.

"Yeah," he said, nodding his head in agreement.

And I'm going to say that to come up with these 30 minority managers some major league teams had to stretch the meaning of the word executive real far, I continued.

For instance, the California Angels listed the team's executive chef and photographer. And the Chicago Cubs said its equipment manager is one of the club's top executives. The White Sox put its clubhouse manager, the guy who is responsible for clean towels and uniforms, on their list, I said.

"Damn. They got some nerve," Ungawah snarled. "But you're well-connected, man. Can't you get brothers and sisters at newspapers 'round the country to beat up on Major League Baseball?"

Uh, well, yeah. We could try to do that, I mumbled.

"What do you mean try, chump?" Ungawah said, his voice quivering. "A third of all baseball players are black. We're good enough to play the game and make some owners rich, but we're not good enough to be an executive on their teams. Man, every black journalist ought to be mad as hell 'bout that."

We are, Ungawah, I answered.

"So why can't you mobilize them and get stories in all the newspapers?" he asked.

Well, Ungawah. It's just not that easy, I said. You see, we've got a little problem. There aren't that many blacks working for newspapers. In fact, compared to the media, baseball doesn't look that bad.

"What you tellin' me, man?" Ungawah asked, breaking stride. "You tellin' me that there are more blacks in baseball than there are in newspapers?"

Percentage-wise, yes, I answered softly. That's what I'm saying. Minorities make up less than four percent of baseball executives; that's about the same percentage of management jobs we hold in the newspaper industry.

Suddenly, Ungawah reached out and snatched the picket sign from my hand.

"Look, brother, I don't need you on my picket line," he said. "I can handle baseball. You need to throw up your own picket line when you get back to the office."

A real terrorist

NEW YORK, Dec. 27, 1988

The sight of my longtime friend and nemesis in the clutches of jail guards ought to have been enough to muddle my emotions, but it wasn't.

To see Ungawah Jones draped in prison garb and shackled like a common thug, standing limply before me with rumpled guards at his side, actually warmed my heart.

Finally, Ungawah was suffering a fate more severe than the many put-downs he had made me endure over the years. Nothing he had ever done to me could match the days Ungawah had just spent in the Rikers Island jail for pure humiliation.

So, what's happening, Ungawah, I said, flashing a wide grin as I surveyed, with obvious delight, the condition of my friend.

"Yo, Shakespeare. Don't come in here with no Cheshire cat grin on your face, man. This ain't 'bout nothin' funny."

Well, I'm sorry if you don't see the humor in this moment, my friend, I responded, but it's not often that I see you so wrapped up in yourself, if you know what I mean.

Ungawah glared at me as my laughter echoed off the walls of the dingy visitors' room.

"All right, geek. Have a laugh on me, but when you finish, get me outta here. I've gotta get back over to the U.N.," he said with the firmness of a man obsessed.

Hold on, Ungawah. I didn't put up your bail just so you can go out and get yourself arrested again. If you're leaving here with me, you're not going anywhere near the United Nations, I answered.

And besides, I continued, where do you get off trying to make a citizen's arrest of a foreign official, Ungawah? You're damn lucky they didn't put you under the jail.

"Look, dummy," Ungawah said in a real huff, "it may be OK with you that that terrorist was allowed to visit the U.N., but it makes me madder than hell."

Terrorist, I said. The man is the South African foreign minister. He was there to sign an agreement that will bring independence to Namibia, Africa's last colony.

"Yeah, well I don't care why he was there, the man is a terrorist, and the South African government is a terrorist organization," Ungawah reasoned. "Man, they wouldn't let that P.L.O. guy Yasser Arafat into the country to address the U.N. — said he was a terrorist."

OK, Ungawah, let's not get caught up in all this terrorism stuff. I just want your assurance that when you get out of here you won't blow my bail money by going back to the U.N. and getting yourself arrested again.

"Chump, I'm not worried 'bout your money. Where's your commitment to the brothers and sisters who are being terrorized by them racists in South Africa?" Ungawah asked.

"You see, that guy George Shultz has a double standard," he continued. "He won't let Arafat come to the U.N. 'cause he says the man's a terrorist. But then he goes to the U.N. and sits down with this dude Botha. Man, when it comes to terrorism, South Africa is the pits."

I'll grant you that, Ungawah. But you can't take the law into your own hands, I said. You just can't storm the U.N. and try to arrest a foreign diplomat. Besides, Pik Botha is back in South Africa by now.

"What? You mean they let him get away?" snapped Ungawah.

What I mean, Ungawah, is . . .

"That's OK, geek," he interrupted, "I don't wanna know what you mean. Just tell me this. Did he renounce terrorism before he left?"

Huh? I winced.

"Did he recognize the right of black South Africans to exist within secure borders?" Ungawah persisted.

No, but . . . were the only words I got out before Ungawah cut me off again.

"Did he say he was willing to negotiate with the African National Congress?" he demanded.

Well, no, I answered softly.

"Did he at least promise to stop torturing black women and children and puttin' them in jail without a trial?" Ungawah asked, more out of frustration than rage.

"Just one more question," Ungawah said. "Does it bother you at all, man, that they stuck me in jail, and not Botha?" The look in his eyes told me he wasn't looking for an answer, just some understanding.

CHAPTER 5
Setting the record straight

ONE of the great American pastimes is the national back-slapping that takes place at the mere mention of a patriotic holiday, or symbol. Like the self-flagellation of Islamic zealots, such behavior says more about a person's gullibility than anything else.

While much is made of American egalitarianism, the record of this country's democracy is a spotty one. Opportunity in this great republic does not beckon huddled masses as did once the Statue of Liberty.

The Fourth of July, the most famous symbol of American independence — and the freedoms most have come to cherish — is a meaningless holiday for some others. Likewise, the Constitution that embodies the basic tenets of our great democratic experiment is not without its flaws.

Getting those who revel in the successes of this nation to acknowledge these and other serious shortcomings is no easy task.

Whether it is the failures of the Founding Fathers, the video voyeurism of a television network or the shortsightedness of a small town's school officials, one thing is certain: We must set the record straight. ■

Setting the record straight

Lady Liberty a Trojan horse

HYDE PARK, N.Y., July 8, 1986

Greek mythology has it that history was forever altered when the people of Troy accepted as a gift a large wooden horse left standing outside the gates of that warring city-state.

Hidden in the bowels of the towering structure, which the admiring Trojans pulled inside their city, were the point men of an invading army. Troy fell within a day.

Back in 1886, the people of France, in a true gesture of friendship, bestowed upon the United States the Statue of Liberty. It was a monument to America's egalitarian spirit. That same year, 74 blacks were lynched in this country.

The contradictions presented by the two events is but one of many reasons why last week's blitz and glitz commemorating the 100th birthday of the Statue of Liberty drew little support, or attention, from blacks — a small group of whom gathered last weekend in this town on the banks of the Hudson River for a Fourth of July cookout.

The assembled were modern-day immigrants, of a sort. None of them were native to this historic community, the longtime home of Franklin D. Roosevelt. Middle-class migrant workers, they were recently of places like Dallas, Philadelphia, Washington and Selma, Ala. As success models, they are among the best that blacks have to offer: The owner of a car dealership, a civil engineer, a newspaper executive and an electronics company manager.

They, more than any other black Americans, should appreciate what the Statue of Liberty represents to a good number of people in this country.

But if they are of a genre of black Americans who have tasted the milk and honey of this land, their memories also are sufficiently long to ward off the euphoria that comes to many whites at the very mention of the

The ships that brought our ancestors to these shores were packed with huddled masses all right, but none of them put in at Ellis Island. Their ports of call were the harbors that trafficked in the slave trade.

Statue of Liberty.

They are not unpatriotic. Like most black Americans, they too have a real love for this country. But they view the Statue of Liberty's multi-million dollar, Fourth of July weekend birthday bash with more than a bit of disdain.

To the extent that they made mention of the lavish ceremonies taking place to the south, at the mouth of the Hudson, they found it odd that the government would spend $70 million to refurbish the monument and then signal the project's completion by loosing thousands of pigeons in the vicinity of Lady Liberty. "Had the pigeons been paper trained?" someone asked.

Beyond this fleeting notice, it was obvious that the Statue of Liberty has little real symbolism for them, or for most black Americans.

The ships that brought our ancestors to these shores were packed with huddled masses all right, but none of them put in at Ellis Island. Their ports of call were the harbors that trafficked in the slave trade.

And even today for those blacks fleeing oppressive conditions in Cuba and Haiti, the reception they receive here is often hostile. Once they set foot in this "land of the free," they are as likely to be imprisoned as greeted with open arms by immigrations officials.

Apparently there is little that offends government officials more than an uninvited black immigrant in search of the American dream.

All of which causes me to wonder what might have happened if the Frenchman who built the Statue of Liberty had been overtaken by his revolutionary fervor. Imagine.

Instead of sending a hollow monument to New York, he could have stuffed the statue full of hundreds of heavily armed African warriors and deposited it in Charleston harbor.

First the city, the state of South Carolina and then the entire South would have fallen in quick order. Think of the snowballing effect such a turn of events might have had on history.

Today Martin Luther King Jr. would be the senior senator from Georgia. Haiti would be a state. Jesse Helms and Strom Thurmond political nonentities, and Ronald Reagan still a second-rate Hollywood actor. And blacks, fully enfranchised, would have found meaning in last week's festivities.

No, the Statue of Liberty was not a Trojan horse, but it should have been.

Video voyeurism

WASHINGTON, Jan. 29, 1986

By now much of America is talking about last weekend's CBS News special, *The Vanishing Family — Crisis in Black America.*

If you didn't see the two-hour broadcast, you missed the latest example of television at its so-called persuasive best. Hosted by Bill Moyers, the program took viewers to the streets of Newark, N.J. — to neighborhoods into which white America almost never ventures, and middle-class blacks long since have abandoned.

It was a report on the national epidemic of births to unwed black teen-agers and the problems brought on by their single-parenting. The show was also an inciting story about the changing definition of the word "family" within the black lexicon.

Television has a way of giving validation to contemporary issues and debates. "The media," as Marshall McLuhan said, "is the message." Still, I sat down to watch Moyers' examination of this problem with more than a bit of contempt. Television, in its own arrogant way, finally had come to acknowledge a problem that many blacks have been combating for years. I wondered where was the major network attention two years ago when 100 black organizations convened a three-day meeting in Nashville to discuss the plight of the black family.

For more than a decade now many black activists have been involved in a kind of trench warfare, doing battle with the problems that afflict the black family.

In 1980 the Children's Defense Fund, a Washington-based non-profit organization, issued a detailed report on the black family crisis. And in its second "State of Black America" report in 1978, the National Urban League focused attention on this problem.

Effective local programs have been developed in several cities as a result to strengthen the black family and reduce incidents of teen-age pregnancy to unwed mothers.

While camera crews have been dispatched all over the globe to chronicle all sorts of news events, seldom have they been sent to the inner cities of America to report on the breakup of the black family — that is, until now.

Bypassing the experts, Moyers went straight to the people affected most. This method, while admirable in concept, in execution resulted in oversimplification of the problem and its possible solutions.

The net result, I suspect, is that many viewers came away with some twisted answers to the basic question: Why are there so many unwed teen-age mothers in the black community, and what can be done about this problem?

Believe me, it's not simply because of the rampaging of over-sexed, unemployed black men, as suggested in the CBS broadcast. And the solution is not as clear-cut as getting rid of welfare.

The damage done by the CBS special is that it leaves viewers with these impressions. Ironically, CBS did not turn its cameras on this "black problem" until the number of teen-age pregnancies among whites began to surge.

According to the National Center for Health Statistics, while black teen-age pregnancies per capita far exceed those of whites, the birth rate for unwed white teens is rising while the rate for black teens is on the decline.

Moyers talked to black unwed mothers and the men who fathered their children. He gave us a look into their lives, a sense of their hopes, frustrations and their despair. It was a kind of video voyeurism that allowed millions of Americans to leer at the victims of this social trage-dy from the safety of their living rooms.

Lost in this report was the broader picture — the considered analysis of cause and effect.

Also not shown were the thousands of black unwed mothers who struggle, but manage to work and provide their children with a decent lifestyle. Not revealed were the many decent black men who play meaningful roles in the lives of the children they spawn out of wedlock.

If answers are to be found to the problems that afflict the black fam-ily, they will surface only after a serious examination of the factors that contribute to the waning sense of self-dignity that pervades the victims in this crisis. Bill Moyers' report was a superficial treatment of the prob-lem.

The CBS News special may have been intended to shed some new light on this very troubling problem, but in truth it has added little of substance to the search for solutions.

If anything, it rendered television's brief intrusion upon this crisis illegitimate.

Setting the record straight

An interview with Martin

WASHINGTON, Jan. 17, 1986

Imagine what it would be like if Martin Luther King Jr. were alive today — if his life had not been snuffed out by an assassin's bullet 18 years ago.

Think for a moment. What would he say? How would he react to the world in which we live and to the events and personalities that shape our lives?

What you are about to read is an interview of Dr. King that never occurred — an interview in which his words are used in response to questions I never got the chance to ask him.

My interview was scheduled for early afternoon at his office in Atlanta's Ebenezer Baptist Church. It was a cold, dreary day, Dr. King's 57th birthday. I arrived a few minutes early and was ushered into a small, cluttered office by one of his aides.

Dr. King walked in a few minutes later. He appeared tired and near exhaustion as he sank slowly into an aging leather chair.

Dr. King, I began, Attorney General Meese has been quoted as saying that in trying to eliminate minority hiring goals for federal contractors he is attempting to bring about the color-blind society you have often talked about. Are you opposed to affirmative action programs as he suggests — programs that use goals, quotas or timetables to remedy past discrimination against black Americans?

Leaning forward and fixing his stare, Dr. King spoke slowly.

"No amount of gold could provide an adequate compensation for the exploitation and humiliation of the Negro," he said. "Yet a price can be placed on unpaid wages . . . The payment should be in the form of a massive program by the government of special compensatory measures which could be regarded as a settlement in accordance with the accepted practice of common law."

Sir, you are aware that President Reagan has been accused by other civil rights leaders of being indifferent to the problems of black Americans, I followed up. Also, that an increasing number of whites believe they are the victims of reverse discrimination. What is your reaction to this situation?

"We may have to repent in this generation not merely for the vitriolic actions and words of the bad people, but also for the appalling silence of good people," he answered. "The black revolution is much more than a struggle for the rights of Negroes. It is forcing America to face all its interrelated flaws — racism, poverty, militarism and materialism."

You are aware, sir, I continued, that there are those in the black community who disagree with you — people who call themselves black conservatives and who say that we must stop pressing the federal government for special programs to aid minorities. What they suggest is needed are more opportunities for blacks to gain economic independence. Do you agree?

"We know from painful experience that freedom is never voluntarily given by the oppressor," Dr. King said. "It must be demanded by the oppressed. The Negro cannot win . . . if he is willing to sell the future of his children for his personal and immediate comfort and safety."

Now, sir, I said, I know that you have watched with interest events in South Africa. Is there a role for black Americans in the freedom struggle of blacks in South Africa?

Rising from his seat, Dr. King walked to a window and looked out at several small children at play.

"We realize that injustice anywhere is a threat to justice everywhere," he began his answer. "Therefore, we are concerned about the problems of Africa as we are about the problems of the United States."

Bishop Desmond Tutu, who had been thought to share your philosophy of non-violent protest, said the other day that there may be a situation where violence is justifiable, I said. In your opinion, is violence ever acceptable as a means of obtaining racial justice?

"Violence as a way of achieving racial justice is both impractical and immoral," he responded, turning away from the window.

"It is impractical because it is a descending spiral ending in destruction for all . . . Violence is immoral because it thrives on hatred rather than love. . . . It creates bitterness in the survivors and brutality in the destroyers."

There was desperation in his voice — an unspoken appeal to accept his logic, his belief in non-violent change.

A patriarch of the civil rights struggle, Dr. King has seen his influence at home and abroad eroded in recent years. In places like Lebanon, Northern Ireland, South Africa, Nicaragua and Iran, more and more people have resorted to violence to settle their conflicts.

At home, black youths have used violence in a perversion of nature's law of the survival of the fittest. Black-on-black crime is depleting their ranks. And in a new form of violence, the Reagan administration has waged an economic war on America's poor and disenfranchised.

Still, Dr. King clings to his belief in non-violent struggle and change — and in the power of right over might.

Once a dreamer, always a dreamer.

Our Founding Fathers

WASHINGTON, July 5, 1987

Imagine this.

The year is 1787 and the place is Philadelphia. Seated among the small clique of white men who wrote the Constitution — men who have come to be known as the Founding Fathers — are some people whose presence history would not record.

They are blacks with names like W.E.B. DuBois, Frederick Douglass and Malcolm X. It matters little that in truth these men were not yet born when the Constitution was written. Just imagine what might have happened had they been part of that historic gathering, if the very words they would speak decades later had been uttered in 1787.

I did.

I can hear the mindless chatter fill the room as delegates to the Constitutional Convention move quickly to deny blacks and women the right to vote in the government they are fashioning. It is DuBois, whose Niagara Movement gave birth to the National Association for the Advancement of Colored People, who first raises his voice in protest.

"No state can be strong which excludes from its wisdom the knowledge possessed by mothers, wives and daughters," the Harvard-trained sociologist argues in favor of giving women the vote.

To permit blacks the vote, DuBois continues, "is absolutely necessary to the realization of the broadest justice for all citizens."

And when the Founding Fathers decide blacks will be counted as only three-fifths of a person in apportioning seats in the House of Representatives, Malcolm X is enraged. He leaps to his feet in obvious disgust.

"I am not an American," he shouts bitterly. "I'm not deluding myself. I'm not going to sit at your table and watch you eat, with nothing on my plate, and call myself a diner. Being born in America doesn't make you an American . . . as long as blacks have been in this country, they aren't Americans yet. They are the victims of Americanism."

It is tough talk from a man who nearly two centuries later would once again rail against the injustices that blacks were made to suffer. He would eventually find widespread support among blacks who saw themselves as the continued "victims of Americanism."

But on this day in 1787, Malcolm X's audience is a small band of white aristocrats — men who are unmoved by his passion and his rage.

It is not until the delegates have completed their drafting of the Constitution and begin to celebrate that the tall, handsome black man seated near the rear of the room rises to speak.

He slowly reads aloud the document's preamble: "We the people of the United States, in order to form a more perfect union, establish justice . . ." The cynicism in his voice cuts through the smoke-filled room with the sting of a Minuteman's musket ball.

"Your celebration is a sham; your boasted liberty, an unholy license; your national greatness, swelling vanity; your sounds of rejoicing are empty and heartless; your denunciation of tyrants, brass-fronted impudence . . . a thin veil to cover up crimes which would disgrace a nation of savages," Frederick Douglass bellows.

Douglass, a moving orator who would become the conscience of the anti-slavery, abolitionist movement, was this day no match for the likes of James Madison and Benjamin Franklin. His protests were drowned out in the celebration of the fledgling nation's new Constitution.

As the Founding Fathers filed out of the room, the three black men sat motionless, immobilized by their knowledge of what the coming years would bring.

Too much for you to imagine?

Well, not me. I often wonder what might have happened if some black voices of reason — and even passion — had been heard by the men who crafted the Constitution.

Maybe this nation could have avoided the enslavement of millions of blacks and a devastating civil war. It could have prevented the lynchings and race riots that took such a heavy human toll.

And most of all, it could have avoided the troubling racial divisions that have plagued us ever since. Imagine that.

Setting the record straight

A real egalitarian act

MIAMI, Aug. 29, 1987

The fix is in. In fact, it has been years in the making.

Later this month this nation will erupt on command in celebration of the 200th anniversary of our Constitution. A document that has come to stand for a lot more than its authors ever intended. The Constitution of these United States will be acclaimed as the great instrument of our freedom. The "our" is much too inclusive.

I know, I'm not supposed to be doing this — raining on Warren Burger's parade — but I can't help myself. Hypocrisy is not something I do well.

C'mon now, give us a break, Warren. Let's get this thing into proper perspective. What happened 200 years ago in Philadelphia was a fluke as far as a good number of Americans are concerned. The Constitution was never intended to include women, blacks or native Americans in the "more perfect union" that the Founding Fathers envisioned. As drafted, it was an elitist document intended to "secure the blessings of liberty" for some, while denying freedom to others.

That it has come to be more than that does not change the original, mean-spirited intent of the small clique of white men whose narrow sense of liberty gave birth to the Constitution. When they wrote the words, "We the people," they were talking about a very select group of folks.

Last week I looked on as Leon Higginbotham, a federal appeals court judge, addressed a gathering at the National Association of Black Journalists convention, here in Miami. He had come to discuss the bicentennial of the Constitution "from a racial perspective" — just the kind of talk that organizers of this month's celebration don't want to hear.

"The Constitution did not provide even a ray of hope that blacks could secure justice through the federal legal system" without the aid of a costly civil war, the black jurist said. Tough talk from a federal judge? Well, there's more.

"The early failure of the nation's founders and their constitutional heirs to share the legacy of freedom with black Americans is the major factor in America's perpetual racial tensions," Higginbotham added.

OK, so the Founding Fathers didn't get it all right. But is that any reason to trash the Constitution's 200th birthday party?

Higginbotham thinks it's OK for the nation to rejoice in the anniversary if people take note of the Constitution's glitches — and the continuing impact they are having on us.

"We do not celebrate or condone the three-fifths clause; we do not celebrate the clause protecting the international slave trade; we do not celebrate or condone the fugitive slave clause ... We do not meet to honor the limited vision" that the Founding Fathers had of the role of women in our society, Higginbotham told his audience.

Instead, we should celebrate the enactment "of the 13th, 14th, 15th and 19th amendments and the related civil rights acts — in which our nation has repudiated, in part, the racism and sexism sanctioned" by the drafters of the Constitution, he added.

In many ways, what Higginbotham suggests begs the question of why blacks and others who were disenfranchised by the Founding Fathers should observe the 200th anniversary of the Constitution with anything other than a black arm band.

Sure, the 13th, 14th, 15th and 19th amendments made it better for blacks and women in this country, but they came many years after the original document was etched into history. And while the Founding Fathers' Constitution made the enactment of these amendments possible, it was never intended by them that their document be altered to end slavery, or give women the vote.

For blacks to take part in this celebration would be an act of self-flagellation — an expression of denial that rivals James Earl Ray's claim of innocence.

I suggest we put away the fireworks and confetti until 2065 when we can celebrate the 200th anniversary of the 13th Amendment — a real egalitarian act.

Misplaced outrage

WASHINGTON, Jan. 8, 1986

I had promised friends I would not join the rush to comment publicly on *The Color Purple,* Alice Walker's Pulitzer Prize-winning book that Steven Spielberg has brought to the silver screen.

I lied.

I told them I did not want to be counted among those persons who have taken this movie too seriously. When I heard people were picketing the movie in Los Angeles — something about it portraying black men negatively — I laughed. Given all of the real injustices that take place daily in this world, I thought that was such a waste of time.

I wondered how many of those movie pickets have pounded the pavements in protest of South Africa's treatment of its black majority, or in opposition to the Reagan administration's cutbacks in domestic spending programs. I thought, probably not many.

Then, last weekend, the ruckus over *The Color Purple* touched me personally. The regular Saturday morning basketball game I look forward to — a competition in which a 6-2 center is a dominating presence, and my waning jump shot is still feared — was called off. The guys wanted to get together instead to talk about the way the movie dumped upon black men. Unbelievable.

I had sat through a showing of the movie *Johnny Dangerously* — along with five other persons who paid to see this celluloid bomb — and I didn't feel moved to call a town meeting to discuss its failings.

I tried several times to call my old friend Oprah Winfrey, one of the stars of *The Color Purple,* to discuss the movie with her. I don't think she would be associated with a film that has no redeeming social value — one that deprecated the black male.

She didn't return my calls. But that's understandable. I can't get Michael Jackson to take my calls either. Celebrity has a way of putting distance between people.

Still, I thought the concerns my friends and other black men raised, in the context of this movie, were frivolous. The charges they leveled against Alice Walker — that her feminist leanings spawned her Pulitzer Prize book, a book they labeled anti-black male — I found hard to accept.

I do not think she is an evil person. A couple of years ago I paid the princely sum of $100 for a copy of Alice Walker's book at a local NAACP celebrity auction. From her home in San Francisco, she was kind enough to inscribe a warm greeting in the book, which she returned to me in short order. I've waited longer for some of my male friends to repay an "overnight" loan.

More importantly, I have seen the movie and read Walker's book. *The Color Purple,* both in print and on the screen, is a compelling story about the triumph of oppressed people over their oppressors.

Walker may have intended it to be a story about good black women overcoming the tyranny of evil black men, but that's not my perception of her work. When I saw the movie, I related to Celie, her main female character and not to Mister, the movie's dominant male figure.

I felt pain for her suffering and I rejoiced in her victories. I was angered by the way the men in her life treated her, but I did not project their actions to the broader group of black men.

Celie was victimized by some of the black men in her life. And as the victim of injustices, she won my sympathy.

When I discussed with a close friend the negative reactions to the movie I was getting from black men, he offered this explanation: "I think that what this points out is the very fragile nature of the black existence in this country. That black men are so ego-sensitive they cannot accept a movie about black male brutality to powerless black women. I think that's a shame."

More than a shame, it's an indication of our failure to keep the world in proper perspective.

At best, *The Color Purple* is a very good movie, but just a movie. I do not accept it as a treatise on life, nor as an empirical study of relationships between black men and women.

To the extent that I am offended, it is because Hollywood so severely restricts the spectrum of black images that moviegoers can see. It bothers me that movie studios won't give some of the many talented black directors a chance to bring a work like *The Color Purple* to the screen.

Beyond that, I save my rage for life's real villains. And in this regard, *The Color Purple* does not merit my attention.

A pregnant cheerleader

JACKSON, Miss., Nov. 3, 1986

Letters to the editor, like lengthy conversations with black conservatives, are things I avoid at all costs. Both tend to offend my egalitarian spirit.

The former are largely devoid of rational thought. The latter can render one a dunderhead. There are, however, rare exceptions.

Take, for example, a letter to the editor that I stumbled upon in *The*

Setting the record straight

(Jackson) *Clarion-Ledger.* It was a bit of angry talk from a mother in nearby Crystal Springs.

She was all worked up over a recent decision by local officials to allow a pregnant teen-ager to be a cheerleader at Crystal Springs High School — to prance about at pep rallies and sporting events turning cartwheels and pumping school spirit.

The complaining mother views this decision as an outrage: "Loose morals and promiscuous behavior are now to be rewarded. What an injustice," she wrote with obvious passion.

To be a cheerleader, the mother argued, is to hold a position of leadership and prestige. To allow a pregnant student to be a cheerleader, she reasons, is to send the wrong message to the student body. Hardly an irrational thought.

Teen-age pregnancy is this nation's latest social crisis. As the number of babies born to unwed teens swells, the fabric of this society tears.

More than 1 million teen-age girls a year become pregnant. About half of them give birth. Teen-age mothers face a greater likelihood of a lifetime of poverty. They are at higher risk of dropping out of school. They are more likely to be unemployed and locked into some sort of public assistance.

Given these realities, discouraging teen pregnancies ought to be constantly on the minds of everyone, including officials in Crystal Springs — egalitarian spirits notwithstanding.

Children in our democratic society have lots of rights, but being a pregnant cheerleader should not be one of them.

Participation in extracurricular activities ought to be a privilege afforded to those schoolchildren whose behavior meets generally accepted community standards.

Denying teen-age girls who become pregnant the privilege of being a school cheerleader — and teen-age fathers the possibility of playing on the school team — may very well serve as a disincentive to such self-destructive behavior.

No, by itself this action will not stem the national tide of teen-age pregnancies, but it represents a move in the right direction. Given the nature of this problem, almost any move is better than none.

Children are not little adults. They are adolescents who are still developing a sense of right and wrong. They are, I suspect, much more susceptible to peer pressures, incentives and disincentives than are adults. So why not make teen-age parenting costly in ways that young-sters can understand?

There is, of course, a danger in all of this.

School systems across this nation have a rather spotty record when it comes to meting out discipline. In cities such as Cincinnati, Seattle, Des Moines and Los Angeles, minority students are more likely to be sus-pended or expelled than are whites.

While some suggest that such disparities are because of higher levels of disruptive behavior among minority students, there are those who say that something else is at work here.

One friend of mine, a public school administrator, argues that many white and black teachers feel threatened by black students, and thus are likely to treat their infractions more harshly than those of whites.

And here's something else to think about.

Among teen-agers who become pregnant, whites are statistically more likely than blacks to have an abortion. Thus by doing what many would say is the morally correct thing to do, black teen-agers who give birth to their babies would suffer the disincentives while those white teens who abort their pregnancies might not.

Of course, a sure way to overcome this disparity is to avoid becom-ing pregnant.

All right, so there are no easy answers. But that's no reason for people not to try to grapple with the growing problem of teen-age pregnancies in this country.

That's what the letter to the editor from the mother in Crystal Springs is all about. The last thing our schools need, she wants us to understand, is pregnant cheerleaders.

And I couldn't agree more.

CHAPTER 6
The politics of reason

POLITICS, like sex and slow-pitch softball, is an American passion. And like those sports played in bedrooms and on sandlots, politics sets forth few restrictions on participants that are worthy of mention.

The ranks of politicians are overrun with scoundrels and political opportunists. Both tend to overshadow and — once in office — outvote their well intentioned colleagues. Getting elected officials to do the right thing is more often than not complicated by the real inability of some to distinguish between right and wrong.

Far too many politicians are overburdened by ideology, party affiliation and personal greed to perform any truly useful services for the constituents they were elected to serve. But there are notable exceptions — people who have succumbed to the politics of reason.

Among those I have written about, Mike Espy is my favorite. A black Democrat who sits in the Mississippi congressional seat once held by Jefferson Davis, Espy won election by galvanizing the black vote and winning the support of a sizable number of whites.

Once while making a big pitch to some of the congressional district's white voters — most of whom are farmers — Espy was asked by a reporter if the economic relief he was seeking for farmers would come at the expense of blacks. "Everybody who eats," he answered smartly, "is involved in agriculture."

But it seems that for every Mike Espy I run across, there exists a Pat Buchanan or an Eddie Vrdolyak — con men of the political variety. Left unchecked, they will do as much damage to the exercise of democratic government here as Pol Pot did to literacy in Cambodia. ■

Do be serious

WASHINGTON, Aug. 16, 1987

It seems there exist some Republican presidential contenders who are unabashed in their quest for black voters, the kind of covetous behavior that only liberal Democrats used to exhibit.

So startling is this revelation that many a journalist has taken to commenting on this bit of news which, for most, has the shock value of a "man bites dog" story.

Senate leader Robert Dole, Rep. Jack Kemp and Vice President George Bush have all been heard to utter yearnings for blacks to come over to the GOP in support of their presidential bids. It wasn't long ago that such open courting of blacks by Republican presidential candidates would cause them to be viewed as less than serious contenders. But not so this presidential season.

Doubtful as I am of their sincerity, I am nonetheless willing to give these three stalwarts of the GOP a chance to prove their good intentions. In fact, I want to help them in their cause.

Thus, I am offering them my list of dos and don'ts for Republican presidential candidates who court the support of black voters:

Do be serious!

Don't lapse into "black English" when talking to blacks.

Do develop a taste for soul food, just as you have learned to stomach pasta, bagels and lox and sushi in your quest for the votes of others.

Don't call chitlins, chitterlings.

Do learn something about black culture.

Don't try to impress blacks by having your hair Jherie-curled.

Do be serious!

Don't quote Martin Luther King Jr.

Do quote Stevie Wonder.

Don't try to win over blacks by seeking an endorsement from Michael Jackson ... Don't invite black Muslim leader Louis Farrakhan to a campaign pig roast. Do ask New York Mayor Ed Koch to come as the guest of honor.

Don't use the U.S. invasion of Grenada as an example of America's military might.

Do call William Shockley a jerk.

Don't take to wearing "jams" at outings with blacks.

Do be serious!

Don't decry welfare.

Do decry government programs that pay farmers not to grow crops.

Don't applaud the actions of Bernhard Goetz.

Do support black majority rule in South Africa.

Don't try to win over blacks by seeking an endorsement from Michael Jackson.

Do be serious!

Don't claim a closeness to Ronald Reagan.

Do distance yourself from the man.

Don't promise to appoint a black to your cabinet.

Do promise to appoint more than one black to your cabinet.

Don't be overheard remarking at a black gathering as to how you would like to cruise to Bimini with Whitney Houston in tow.

Do be serious!

Don't hire Pat Buchanan for any reason.

Do pledge to meet regularly with black leaders both before and after you are elected.

Don't use basketball player Magic Johnson, baseball star Reggie Jackson or William "The Refrigerator" Perry, of the Chicago Bears football team, to tout your campaign.

Do try to get economist Andrew Brimmer, National Education Association head Mary Futrell and Alvin Poussaint, the Harvard psychiatrist, to say something good about your candidacy.

Don't go to Glady's Soul Food restaurant on Chicago's South Side and order filet mignon.

Do promise to fire Brad Reynolds.

Don't invite black Muslim leader Louis Farrakhan to a campaign pig roast.

Do ask New York Mayor Ed Koch to come as the guest of honor.

Don't let Sammy Davis Jr. embrace you in front of television cameras.

Do be serious!

Don't go on the Phil Donahue show and talk about workfare.

The politics of reason

Do go on the Oprah Winfrey show and talk about workfare.

Don't campaign in poor black neighborhoods and talk about how you grew up poor, too.

Do really get to know some black folks.

Don't tell black kids that one day they might grow up to be president of the United States.

Do be serious!

The 'R' word

WASHINGTON, Oct. 26, 1988

Backers of Democratic presidential candidate Michael Dukakis thought they were onto something when they began to moan their objections to the menacing television image of Willie Horton.

Instinctively, these campaign insiders — who relish political redemption in much the same way a butcher delights in gutting a hog — started to use the "R" word.

It was "racist," they charged, for supporters of GOP presidential candidate George Bush to air television ads that attacked their man as being soft on crime by projecting Horton's black face into the living rooms of millions of white Americans.

And it was an act of political survival for the people behind Dukakis to label the action with the one word that could convince black voters to turn out in large numbers on Election Day.

Horton is a convicted murderer who walked away from a weekend prison furlough program in Massachusetts and then raped a white woman.

Dukakis' supporters understand that few offenses inflame racial passions more than the rape of a white woman by a black man. That Horton was free to commit this violation of white womanhood is to be blamed on Dukakis, Massachusetts' governor, the Bush camp contends.

Coming as it did in the wake of a successful Republican campaign to brand Dukakis as a liberal who is far to the left of most Americans, the ad is less than subtle.

"The issue isn't Willie Horton," a Bush aide explained. "The issue is why did he get out and why didn't Michael Dukakis stop it."

Left unexplained, though, is why it was necessary for Bush supporters to broadcast Horton's surly image into the homes of millions of Americans to make their point — the point the campaign publicly admits to, that is.

The answer is simple. The people behind George Bush are unwilling to settle for a narrow win when the prospect of a landslide victory looms large. And the Willie Horton story was just what they needed to rally larger numbers of white voters around their candidate.

Winning white votes is what the Bush campaign is all about. George Bush does not campaign in this nation's black communities, nor has he made a direct pitch to the more than 20 million eligible black voters.

His campaign strategy is influenced more by the meager support Ronald Reagan found among black voters in 1984 — just 9 percent — than by the fact that in 1960 Richard Nixon mounted a campaign that won 32 percent of the black vote.

There's no doubt about it, when the media specialists around Bush put together the commercial with Willie Horton's face staring out at television viewers, they intended to appeal to the racial fears of white voters.

But for the Dukakis camp to charge the Bush campaign with racist behavior seems more than a bit self-serving, if not disingenuous.

Let's face it, in this election campaign Dukakis has put forth only slightly more effort to court black voters than has Bush. While the Republican candidate has written off the black vote, his Democratic rival has taken it for granted.

When the Massachusetts governor was riding high in the polls he made little mention of the issues that arouse black voters. Dukakis was so obsessed with the presidential campaign of Jesse Jackson that he conceded the black vote to the Baptist minister in much the same way that Bush now concedes it to him.

After he won the Democratic nomination, Dukakis continued to bypass black campaign stops in the hope that he might shake off the liberal tag he acquired from the Bush campaign.

And now with the election just a few days off and the polls suggesting that Bush is pulling away, the Democratic candidate has found in the Willie Horton ad a reason to court the black vote.

Michael Dukakis hopes that outraged black voters will go to the polls on Nov. 8 in record numbers and help him defeat George Bush.

His belated appeal to blacks is the last desperate gasp of a troubled campaign.

Pat Buchanan for president

WASHINGTON, Jan. 25, 1987

Patrick Buchanan is not a candidate for the presidency of these United States. That's got to be reassuring news to those who want to preserve this republic.

Not since the misadventures of Aaron Burr — the vice president who plotted in 1804 to seize parts of Mexico and declare himself emperor — has this nation had more reason to fear a politician.

Last week Buchanan ended his brief flirtation with the race for the 1988 GOP presidential nomination. In doing so he left the rabid fringe of the Republican Party's right wing without a true candidate. It will now have to make do with Jack Kemp, a right-of-center Republican whose rabid credentials are suspect.

As for Buchanan, a devotee of Richard Nixon, Spiro Agnew and, more recently, Ronald Reagan, the record is indisputable. The man has little tolerance for democratic process, and an unabashed dislike for those who do not share his world vision.

He suggests that those who oppose aid to the Nicaraguan Contras are soft on communism. Those in Congress who criticize the president belong to a "tribe of pygmies." And he compares the alleged misdoings of former National Security Council staffers Oliver North and John Poindexter to the "moral" acts of people who helped blacks escape from slavery.

"It is not whether some technical laws were broken, but whether we stop communism in Central America," he said last month in defense of the alleged transfer of profits from the Iran arms sale to Nicaraguan rebels. His denials to the contrary, it seems Buchanan believes that the ends justify the means.

To Buchanan, the only good American is one who subscribes to his right-wing conservative doctrine — one who is obsessed with the great ogre of world communism.

And worst of all, Buchanan, who serves Reagan as White House communications director, has even less respect for the media that spawned him — an institution that he uses so adroitly for personal fortune and political gain. What an ingrate.

When Nixon ran for re-election back in 1972, it was Buchanan who offered his campaign staff this bit of advice: "It is very important in terms of the final campaign that the media be effectively discredited."

Discrediting the media is something at which Buchanan has worked awfully hard during his two stints on the White House staff. As speech writer for Spiro Agnew, he wrote some of the vice president's most vicious attacks on newspaper and television organizations thought to oppose Nixon administration policies.

As a defender of Ronald Reagan's handling of the Iran arms sale scandal, he has once again tried to paint the media as the villain for reporting the unpleasant details of the administration's botched effort to secure the release of U.S. hostages in Lebanon.

"All newsmen should remember that they're Americans first and newsmen second," he said recently in attacking the media's coverage of the affair.

Buchanan's notion of patriotism, it seems, is based on blind allegiance to his conservative ideology. Still, no one will ever accuse Buchanan of being unrelenting in his disdain for the media.

Between his stints in the Nixon-Ford and Reagan White House, Buchanan busied himself writing a syndicated column, giving speeches and appearing on network television, for which he reportedly earned upwards of $400,000 annually. So much for conscience.

Having seized the stage late last year in defense of the embattled president, Buchanan quickly found the national spotlight intoxicating. He began to see himself as a possible successor to Ronald Reagan — he fancied himself at the helm of our ship of state, a thought that for me conjures up visions of the Titanic.

Fortunately for all, his illusion was short-lived. When Buchanan announced last week that he was quitting the GOP race, he said he was standing down so as not to "mortally wound" Jack Kcmp's chanccs of winning the party's nomination.

Whatever the reason, it is reassuring to know Buchanan no longer aspires to national office in our government, one based on the rule of law and tolerance of political differences.

Run, Jesse, run

ATLANTA, July 20, 1988

It was hours before Jesse Jackson was to offer what many thought would be the major address of the Democratic National Convention, and Rims Barber already had passed judgment.

"This is the culmination of a lot of dreams, and maybe a few nightmares," he said as he looked across the many rows of empty seats to the stage from which Jackson would speak.

It mattered little that he did not know what Jackson would say. This white man from Mississippi was certain of the speech's impact.

For Barber, a Jackson delegate, and thousands of other people who later crammed into the Omni Coliseum, the words were less important than the event. Jackson was to be the keynote speaker at a political convention that he had come to dominate, and Barber knew the moment would be special.

"For the first time America actually considered the thought that a black man might be president," he said, his words punctuated by his slow speech.

"Once you think about something once, then it is no longer a queer idea . . . and so today's dreams and nightmares are able to become tomorrow's realities."

Four years ago, Jesse Jackson sought the Democratic Party's presidential nomination. Then he was seen as a protest candidate, his Rainbow Coalition consisting almost entirely of black voters. Much has changed since 1984.

This year he mounted a campaign for the White House that won him the backing of nearly 7 million voters in primaries. His support among white voters tripled. And, if only for a fleeting moment after his surprising victory in Michigan, many other white Americans were forced to consider seriously the possibility of a black president.

When party officials slated him for a keynote address at this convention, it was in recognition of his growing influence among Democratic voters.

As the time neared for Jackson to speak, the restless crowd was pregnant with expectation. The floor of the arena was transformed into a sea of red and white posters that carried just the single word: "Jesse!" Near the foot of the speaker's platform, three white men unfurled a large banner proclaiming "Farmers for Jackson," in silent tribute to his growing constituency.

Then as Ray Charles was heard to sing *America the Beautiful,* Jackson made his way to the podium as delegates cheered the arrival of this man who has become in this election year the conscience of the Democratic Party.

For the moment it seemed there was nothing that divided Jackson from those assembled before him, a majority of whom would vote the next day to name Michael Dukakis as the party's presidential nominee.

Jesse Jackson had waged a surprisingly effective campaign to become this nation's first black president. And while he came up short of his goal, this night the delegates were of no mind to treat him like a defeated candidate.

It was a scene I thought America would never reveal in my lifetime. There was a slight tremble in my hand as my pen sought to capture the essence of this historic event. My eyes were made wet by a surge of emotions.

Back in 1975 I was in Cincinnati when a small group of blacks unsuccessfully tried to get Rep. Ronald Dellums to lead them in a third-party bid for the presidency. The members of the National Black Political Assembly were convinced that blacks would never be considered for the nation's highest office by either of the major political parties.

On this night the California congressman stood near me on the convention floor as Jackson spoke, his eyes fixed approvingly on the man at the podium.

"He has made every effort to be inclusive and to move from protest to mainstream politics," Barber had said earlier in the day. Now it was Jackson's chance to plead his cause.

"We meet tonight at a crossroads, a point of decision. Shall we expand, be inclusive, find unity and power, or suffer division and impotence?" Jackson asked rhetorically.

"The greater good," he offered in answer to his question, "is the common good." His was an appeal to the broad spectrum of those who call themselves Democrats — a challenge to the ideological left and right to scck a "common ground" in the fall campaign for the White House. Jesse Jackson the country preacher had now become the political teacher.

And when he was done, the arena erupted in celebration. Music played. Songs were sung, and the stage parted in front of Jackson as hundreds of his supporters surged forward in an effort to meet their candidate for the presidency of these United States.

"It was just fantastic," Barber said to me over the din. "I'm exhausted now but I can't wait to get out there and start campaigning . . . " His last words were drowned out by the noise.

Later I would wonder whether he was talking about this year's general election, or some future presidential campaign of Jesse Louis Jackson.

Phone call away

WASHINGTON, Aug. 24, 1988

George Bush could be just a telephone call away from the presidency.

That's right. If history is any judge, the Republican presidential candidate might be able to secure his victory in the November general election for little more than the price of a long distance telephone call.

All Bush needs to do is ring up South Africa's ruling despot, P.W. Botha, and make an appeal for the release of Nelson Mandela. The imprisoned black nationalist, who has been in jail for 26 years, is now in a South African hospital suffering from tuberculosis.

For many blacks in this country and abroad, Mandela is the dominant symbol of the freedom struggle of South Africa's oppressed black majority. He continues to be the titular head of the black liberation struggle that resulted in his 1962 imprisonment, and subsequent 1964 treason conviction.

It is not unprecedented for a U.S. presidential candidate to use political persuasion, and the media attention he commands, to free a jailed black activist.

In the waning days of the 1960 presidential campaign, John Kennedy placed a much publicized telephone call to the wife of Martin Luther King Jr. while his aides scurried behind the scenes to win the release of the black civil rights leader from a Georgia jail cell.

King had been arrested for his part in a non-violent civil rights demonstration, the kind Mandela used to engage in before the brutal response of South African security police forced him to change his tactics.

Upon his release from jail, King told waiting journalists he "was deeply indebted to Kennedy" — a public pronouncement many historians now credit for a sizable shift of blacks away from the GOP and into the Democratic column on Election Day.

Even King's father, himself an influential Southern black leader and lifelong Republican, threw his support behind the Massachusetts senator's campaign. And, publicly, King expressed his disappointment over Richard Nixon's failure to come to his aid.

"I really considered him a moral coward," King said.

In losing the 1960 election, Nixon won just 32 percent of the black vote, as compared to the 39 percent Dwight Eisenhower pulled four years earlier in his successful re-election bid.

Kennedy defeated Nixon by fewer than 250,000 votes.

Earlier this month, Bush and a few of his Republican cohorts talked generously about pulling blacks into the GOP fold. A shift to the Republicans of 7 percent or more this year could win the election for Bush.

And, unlike Kennedy, Bush would be placing little at stake in such an undertaking.

In 1960, Kennedy's telephone call threatened to further weaken his support among white Southern voters, a good number of whom had already found the Democratic candidate's Catholic religion and liberal views reason enough to vote Republican.

The only thing Bush would risk by summoning Botha to the phone is the ire of the fringe elements of the GOP. These party fanatics have little choice but to vote for Bush, or risk ceding the election to Democrat Michael Dukakis, an unthinkable act for any true-blood Republican conservative.

There is, however, much to be gained by Bush from such a modest act.

He would undoubtedly attract more black voters to his side than Ronald Reagan was able to do. In 1980 Reagan won 12 percent of the black vote. By 1984 his black voter support had fallen to a sorry 9 percent.

Given what is expected to be a close race this year, a shift of almost any discernible number of blacks from the Democratic to the Republican column could spell victory for the GOP ticket.

Whether or not Bush seizes this made-to-order chance to court the black vote will tell us a lot about this presidential candidate who has thus far had few "take charge" opportunities in his long political career.

For the price of a three-minute telephone call to South Africa's state president, George Bush might be able to spring Nelson Mandela from jail and propel himself into the White House.

That's not a bad return on a $4.43 investment.

The Republican option

WASHINGTON, July 13, 1988

The time has come for black voters to consider the Republican option.

While such an idea might seem blasphemous to millions of blacks who have invested all of their political capital in the party of Franklin Roosevelt and Jefferson Davis, it is an option that can no longer be ignored.

For far too long black Americans have been sheep-like in our dedication to the Democratic Party, opting to support all but the most bigoted candidates over any Republican opposition. This blind allegiance has won blacks the label of the Democrats' "most loyal constituency," but no political victories of comparable worth.

Of this nation's 26 Democratic governors there is not a single black. None of the 54 Democrats who serve in the U.S. Senate is black — in fact, of the three blacks who have served in the Senate, two during Reconstruction and one this century, all were Republicans. The political aspirations of black Democrats have been capped at the level of city hall and the House of Representatives — election to which, with few exceptions, comes in political districts dominated by blacks. In other words, black voter support of the Democratic Party has resulted only in that which we have been capable of doing for ourselves, our unflinching party loyalty notwithstanding.

To say that we have been taken for granted by party officials is a gross understatement. To explain why we have clung so long to the political skirts of Democrats would require painful self-analysis. What is becoming clear, however, to a growing number of blacks, is that we need to lift our self-interests above those of the Democratic Party.

More than a decade ago, actor Ossie Davis addressed a meeting of the Congressional Black Caucus and offered its members this admonition:

"We have no permanent friends. We have no permanent enemies. We just have permanent interests."

It is a warning that has been lost upon millions of black voters who have checked little more than a candidate's party affiliation before casting their ballots.

This is not a call for blacks to leave the Democratic fold en masse for the still questionable embrace of the Republicans. The party of Abraham Lincoln, we must always remember, is also the party of Ronald Reagan.

No political strategy that simply involves a decision to vote as indiscriminately for Republicans as we have voted for Democrats can serve our best interests. What we must do is shed the largely unproductive label that our support of Democratic candidates has brought us.

Black voters have got to begin to make intelligent decisions about political candidates that go beyond party considerations. We must be open to the possibility that a George Bush may offer us greater rewards for our vote than a Michael Dukakis.

This year two blacks will compete for U.S. Senate seats in November's general election, one in Maryland and the other in Virginia. Both men are running on the Republican ticket. Two years ago Michigan Republicans nominated Bill Lucas, a black county executive, as their gubernatorial candidate. Though unsuccessful, his campaign demonstrated that the GOP has a greater willingness than do Democrats to offer up blacks for major political office.

There is no sorrier example of the Democrats' abuse of their black constituency than the treatment Jesse Jackson has received in this year's presidential campaign.

The black Baptist preacher finished first or second in 46 of the Democratic primaries and caucuses. He won almost 7 million votes, and his massive voter registration efforts in the past are credited with electing a Democratic majority to the Senate in 1986. And he, more than any other person, will be called upon to get out the vote in November's presidential election.

Yet for all this, Jackson was not even afforded a timely telephone notification from Michael Dukakis of his selection of Texas Sen. Lloyd Bentsen as his vice presidential running mate — a position that Jackson had courted.

For strategists in the Dukakis campaign the "Jackson factor" was of little real consequence in picking a running mate for the Massachusetts governor. More important to them are their efforts to pull less committed white Southern voters back into the party fold, an effort that gave birth to the Dukakis-Bentsen ticket.

Given all of this, black voters must now decide the true value of being the Democratic Party's "most loyal constituency."

Yazoo Mike

YAZOO CITY, Miss., Oct. 20, 1986

"Business is kind of slow," the small black woman complained as she moved out from behind the dimly lit bar. "Sometimes it be a few people here. Sometimes it don't be."

It was 7 p.m., and there was not a single customer in the "Out of Sight Club," a black-owned juke joint in this Mississippi Delta town.

"Sometimes I'm home by 9 o'clock," Roosevelt Fountain said, explaining that when business is real slow he and his wife, Louida, close the club early. "Times are kinda hard right now."

In fact, times are downright miserable for a good number of people throughout the Mississippi Delta, where nearly everyone depends on the farm industry for survival. Caught up in the squeeze brought on by the rapid growth of the federal budget deficit and the nation's foreign trade policies, Delta farmers are struggling to survive.

And when farmers struggle, everyone in the Mississippi Delta feels the pain — a point that Michael Espy keeps driving home to people around here.

Espy, a black Yazoo City lawyer, is the Democratic candidate for Mississippi's Second District congressional seat. His opponents in next month's general election are Republican incumbent Webb Franklin and something that votes alone cannot overcome — the century-old aversion that Mississippi whites have for black office-seekers.

To win next month's general election, Espy must overcome both.

"We have to maximize the black turnout and get a bigger share of the white vote," Espy said. Two years ago, when black Democratic candidate Robert Clark lost to Franklin, only 56 percent of the district's black voters went to the polls. Clark won 12 percent of the white vote.

Espy, whose district is 58 percent black, says he needs the black turn-out to exceed 60 percent and must win close to 20 percent of the white vote to become the first black to represent Mississippi in Congress since Reconstruction.

To pull off his victory, Espy is doing what many black office-seekers outside of the deep South find unproductive, if not unpalatable. He is making an unabashed appeal for white votes. In Mississippi's Second District, that means courting farmers.

The federal government should "guarantee" farmers a profit, Espy said during a meeting with the editorial board of the *Jackson Clarion-Ledger* and the *Jackson Daily News.*

"Thirty percent of our farmers are going bankrupt, and a third more are in real trouble," he said. "We've got to give them some breathing room."

What Espy wants for farmers is a one-year interest-payment morato-rium and a restructuring of their debt.

The policies of the Reagan administration, he said, "seem to favor the real wealthy states over the rural states" — the kind of offense that caused the South to open fire on Fort Sumter 125 years ago.

When it comes to the plight of Mississippi farmers, Espy has learned to "talk that talk." But not, he says, at the expense of blacks.

Espy argues that what's good for farmers is good for everybody in the Second District. "Everybody who eats is involved in agriculture," he quipped.

Mike Espy is part of the new breed of Southern politician. Both black and white, they are men and women willing to forge some political accommodations to break with the past.

For example, told that his opponent had branded him a liberal, Espy responded by saying: "I'm practical, not liberal."

When Hiram Eastland, one of two whites Espy defeated in the pri-mary, endorsed the black candidate, he made mention of Espy's less tangible opponent.

"We've got to quit tiptoeing around the race issue in the South . . . I think we've got to put aside our differences because there is such a tre-mendous amount of common problems that are not separated by race," said Eastland, the cousin of former Mississippi Sen. James O. Eastland.

Espy has been endorsed by nearly all of the top Democratic officeholders in the state, but the test will come Nov. 4, when voters go to the polls in the heavily Democratic Second District.

"I haven't known a black to get a lot of white votes," Peter Harris said as he stood outside of Scott's Barber Shop, just off Main Street in Yazoo City.

"The white farmers are really hurtin', maybe enough to vote for Mike. But I think it's just no way in the world that a lot of white folks will vote for a black man in my lifetime. But I hope I'm wrong."

So does Mike Espy.

Fast Eddie

CHICAGO, April 1, 1987

Politicians in this town are known as much for their bluster as for their ability to coax voters, long since dead, to cast ballots on Election Day.

Forcing the departed to commit a political act in Chicago — even if in name only — ought to be a sin of unforgivable proportions, something akin to voting for mayor of Sodom and Gomorrah.

But subjecting those who live and breathe in this town to the bluster of politicians, particularly that of one Edward Vrdolyak, is no less an offensive act.

"Fast Eddie," as he is called, is a man of many hats. He is chairman of the once powerful Cook County Democratic organization — the one former Mayor Richard J. Daley used to delight in running. He is a Democratic committeeman and an alderman in the Chicago City Council.

A lawyer by training, Eddie Vrdolyak is an opportunist by profession.

His many near misses with the criminal justice system range from an indictment 27 years ago for assault with intent to commit murder to a 1983 accusation of influence peddling.

Most of Vrdolyak's alleged misdeeds evolve around money. But, he has never been convicted of any crimes.

"I treat everybody as if they are wired," Vrdolyak once told a reporter. "I treat everybody like they are wearing a mike."

A remnant of the old Daley machine, Vrdolyak was thought by

many to be destined for the political scrap heap when the reform-minded Harold Washington won election as mayor back in 1983.

But within days of the election of Washington — Chicago's first black mayor — Fast Eddie convinced 28 of Chicago's 50 aldermen to join him in forming a voting bloc in opposition to the new mayor.

For nearly three years the "Vrdolyak 29," as they came to be called, blocked every major initiative of the Washington administration. The City Council was about as racially divided as Chicago's posh Gold Coast neighborhood is from the nearby Cabrini-Green public housing project.

It was not until last year when four Washington allies won council seats in a special election that the mayor was able to control enough votes to push through his programs.

But Harold Washington's victory would be short-lived, Vrdolyak could be heard telling all who would listen.

Washington's election as mayor, he said, had been a political fluke. One of three Democrats vying for the party's nomination in the 1983 campaign, Washington was the only black in the race.

While he won nearly all of Chicago's black votes in the primary, his two white opponents split the white vote in a city where blacks make up nearly 40 percent of the population. Washington went on to defeat his Republican opponent in the general election.

Asked once if Washington would be re-elected, Fast Eddie leaned heavily on his bluster to answer: "Yeah, if he runs unopposed."

But in February, Harold Washington defeated one-time mayor Jane Byrne in the Democratic primary. And on April 7, he will face three challengers in the general election. Democrats all, they are running under other banners in a whimsical effort to unseat the black mayor.

Among these challengers is Eddie Vrdolyak, who has anointed himself as the candidate of the Illinois Solidarity Party. Cook County Assessor Thomas Hynes is wearing the mantle of something called the Chicago First Party, and erstwhile Democrat Donald Haider is the GOP candidate for mayor.

Both the polls and the political arithmetic in this city suggest Washington easily will win election to a second term.

Bluster aside, Fast Eddie will not only lose his bid for the mayoralty come April 7, he will also lose his hold on what remains of the old Daley machine.

The politics of reason

Already, many of the white aldermen who lined up behind him four years ago in opposition to Washington are now expected to throw their support to the black mayor after he is re-elected. And it is rumored that Vrdolyak soon will lose his chairmanship of the Cook County Democratic Party organization.

In the game that is Chicago politics, where bluster and dead voters are standard fare, nothing is as forgettable as a loser — a lesson Fast Eddie Vrdolyak is about to learn.

CHAPTER 7
The gendarmes of apartheid

OUTH Africa is a thug among nations — a pigmentocracy that is dominated by a brutal white minority. The country's black majority is denied the most basic rights and privileges of citizenship, a fact that has caused much of the world to groan its displeasure.

Oppression is not for the weak of heart or stomach. To maintain its control over blacks, the leaders of South Africa's white-racist government have loosed the nation's security forces upon women and children, as well as the men who resist the apartheid system. Rape, torture and murder are used as effectively as banning orders to silence the protests of blacks.

Those who enforce the status quo in South Africa are men and women who comprise the gendarmes of apartheid. To them, an 11-year-old stone-throwing boy is as much a threat as the soldiers of the African National Congress.

There is little that is rational about the behavior of these people. When Eric Sambo accidentally backed a tractor over his employer's dog, the black farmhand was tortured to death by the young white farmer.

Exposing the ugly brutality of this racist state is my obsession. Subjecting the gendarmes of apartheid to the scrutiny and rage of my readers is the very least I can do to help bring an end to this racist state. ■

The gendarmes of apartheid

A despotic act

WASHINGTON, May 27, 1986

The final acts of despotic governments often defy logic. They are predictable only in that they signal the coming apocalypse to their reign of terror.

Last week the racist regime of South Africa launched military raids against targets in Botswana, Zambia and Zimbabwe. The attacks defied logic. The strikes were directed at the African National Congress, the black liberation group committed to dismantling apartheid — the oppressive system used to subjugate South African blacks to the rule of that nation's white minority.

This military action came even as a seven-member British Commonwealth delegation was in South Africa trying to promote talks between the Pretoria government and the ANC.

The damage done by South Africa's marauding forces resulted in greater injury to the government's already badly tarnished image on the world stage than to ANC targets. South African forces reportedly killed three persons in the raids and destroyed several buildings, thought to house ANC activists — actions that were widely condemned here and abroad.

Some suggest last week's raids came in reaction to the South African government's need to demonstrate to white militants that despite recent concessions to blacks — such as repeal of the pass laws — it still is willing to strike anywhere in defense of apartheid.

However, it is South Africa's faltering economy, more than anything else, that is tearing at the fabric of its apartheid government. With at least 30 foreign banks refusing to make new loans to the Pretoria government and the U.S.-led divestment movement gnawing away at foreign corporate investments, South Africa's economy is having

Without foreign capital, or corporate investments — the fuel that powers apartheid's engines — South Africa's racist regime cannot last long.

convulsions. The government cannot pay its short-term debt, and unemployment is on the rise. The bottom is beginning to fall out of the rand.

This financial crisis is brought on by South Africa's racial instability. Banks care less about politics and morality than they do stability. They want some assurances their investments in South Africa are safe. And right now South Africa can't give that to them.

And the economic squeeze in which South Africa finds itself is tightening. More than 40 U.S. cities have restrictions on investments with companies doing business in South Africa.

Already Philadelphia and Washington have pulled their investments ($57 million and $35 million, respectively) out of companies doing business in the racist state.

Other cities that have not yet acted have sizable assets at stake. For instance, New York has $2.1 billion, Baltimore $238 million and Tucson, Ariz., $18 million invested in corporations that financially undergird South Africa's apartheid government.

The U.S. divestment movement also has targeted the purchasing policies of major cities. Earlier this year, San Francisco passed an ordinance barring city purchasing agents from spending more than $5,000 per year with companies that have any ties with South Africa.

New York has a similar law, and Washington and Los Angeles are considering enacting such legislation.

To date, companies like Winn-Dixie, Bell & Howell, Eastman Kodak, Motorola and the Marriott Corp. have stopped doing business with South Africa.

Without foreign capital, or corporate investments — the fuel that powers apartheid's engines — South Africa's racist regime cannot last long.

Its apocalypse is near.

Making peace with the dead

DANIA, Fla., April 29, 1986

It is to cemeteries that the living go to make their final peace with the dead —sometimes, but not always.

The gendarmes of apartheid

On Sunday, officials of the city of Dania went to a local cemetery to right a decades-old wrong — to make their peace with untold numbers of blacks, long since dead.

They were there to dedicate a memorial in memory of the blacks whose bodies in 1940 were removed, unceremoniously, from the corner of the then-integrated city-owned cemetery, to the newly created segregated — "colored" — burial ground.

No one knows the actual number of graves that were disturbed, but for years the tombstones of nearly two dozen blacks whose bodies were moved lay piled on the edge of Dania's "colored" cemetery.

The two burial grounds sit a stone's throw apart, separated by a railroad track, a highway, and the distance that racial bigotry puts between people.

On Sunday, officials of this city of 14,000, a third of whom are black, dedicated a granite memorial — near where the uprooted tombstones once were dumped — to the memories of those whose graves were disturbed. Shortly after the ceremony began, it was over. The city of Dania had made peace with those it victimized 46 years ago.

"I grew up with a lot of animosity in my heart because of this," Marvin Merritt said shortly before the memorial ceremony. "Now, we can put all of this behind us."

The body of his older brother, who died at age nine, was exhumed with the others in 1940. There is no grave marking for it in the "colored" cemetery.

"This city is actively trying to improve its image," said Michael Smith, Dania's personnel director and the man city commissioners assigned to oversee the memorial project. "We have a good image, and we're trying to make it better."

A week earlier in South Africa, officials of the Transkei, a nominal homeland for blacks, were not worrying about "image" when they buried the body of Sabata Dalindyebo, a tribal chief.

Of the 350 "mourners" at the hastily arranged funeral, many carried Uzi machine guns and were dressed in riot gear. Underneath they wore the uniforms of the police and army of the Transkei.

Absent from the grave site were members of the dead chief's immediate family. They were not invited to the funeral. The armed men were present to keep away other uninvited "mourners."

Dalindyebo was a popular leader of the Xhosa tribe and a vocal opponent of South Africa's policy of creating separate homelands for its majority-black population.

In South Africa, a nation where most large gatherings among blacks are banned, funerals take on special significance. The funeral of Dalindyebo, who spent the last nine years of his life in exile, was expected to attract tens of thousands of blacks from across South Africa.

Despotic governments cannot stand such shows of popular support, even for the dead. His body was seized by Transkei officials and hurriedly buried. The court order his family had secured to prevent just such an action was ignored.

A spokesman for the United Democratic Front, the largest anti-apartheid coalition in South Africa, called the government's action a "criminal act of body-snatching."

The leaders of the government of the Transkei, and their mentors in Pretoria, will have to make their peace with Dalindyebo at some later date.

During slavery, many blacks in the American South used to reassure each other that in death they would find freedom from their oppressors. It was a common theme in the Negro spirituals sung during that time. "Soon I will be done with the troubles of the world," intones the words of one such hymn.

That peace, however, is not guaranteed.

It took the good people of Dania 46 years to let many of its black dead rest in peace. But in death, an ocean away, Sabata Dalindyebo is not done with the troubles of the world.

What a pity.

Mimicking apartheid

WASHINGTON, June 4, 1988

The similarities are scary.

In South Africa, government security forces use live ammunition and tear gas to beat back that nation's protesting black majority. Left strewn in their wake are the mutilated and lifeless bodies of those demonstrators who took to the streets in defiance of the white-minority government.

The gendarmes of apartheid

Last year more than 280 black protesters died while confronting the gendarmes of apartheid. Armed mostly with sticks and stones, many of the dead were children.

In Israel's occupied territories, government troops also use fatal force to quiet the protests of the Palestinian-majority they dominate. In the five weeks since the demonstrations began, 27 Palestinians have been killed by Israeli soldiers trying to break up stone-throwing mobs. Many of the dead there, too, were children.

News of these events is increasingly hard to come by as the governments of both countries have blocked the media's coverage of the demonstrations. In South Africa, foreign journalists who violate that nation's press restrictions are usually deported. In Israel recently, a television cameraman was beaten by Israeli soldiers when he tried to photograph six troops assaulting a Palestinian youth.

For years a major supplier of arms to South Africa's embattled white-racist government, Israel is now resorting to tactics honed by the fanatics in Pretoria to suppress the demonstrations of the people of the West Bank and Gaza Strip — the kind of demonstrations the Israelis once engaged in to bring about the creation of the Jewish state.

Pass cards, once required of every black South African, now must be carried by Palestinians in the occupied territories. And while government officials in South Africa continue to use banning orders to silence the most influential black protesters, Israeli officials are threatening to deport Palestinian protest leaders.

Sadly, Israel's use of South African tactics to subdue Palestinian protesters is bad news as much for black South Africans as it is for Arabs in the occupied territories.

Those who opposed the white-minority government of South Africa have tried for years to isolate the apartheid state — to strip away its support in the world community. The call for economic sanctions and arms embargoes are but part of a broader effort to subject South Africans to international condemnation.

By mimicking the behavior of the government in Pretoria, Israeli leaders make it increasingly difficult for the United States to treat the South Africans more sternly without being pressured to act in a similar way toward Israel — something that successive U.S. governments have shown little real willingness to do.

Also, both Israel and South Africa depend heavily on the U.S. for their economic lifeblood. While South Africa continues to depend on U.S. corporations to fuel the economic engines of apartheid, Israel is kept afloat by the more than $3 billion in foreign aid it receives from this country each year.

But it is just such linkages between South Africa and Israel that are beginning to draw the criticism of many black Americans who have grown increasingly weary of relations between the two nations.

Last year the State Department reported that Israel shipped arms to South Africa in violation of United Nations sanctions. And there are those who charge that Israeli experts have aided South Africa in the development of a nuclear bomb.

Given all of this, it won't take long before some anti-apartheid groups begin to view the state of Israel with the same disdain they now hold for those U.S. corporations that continue to operate inside South Africa.

No one should read this to mean that I am anti-Semitic, although surely some will.

The point I am trying to make here is this: Any nation that reacts to the democratic aspirations of a people with guns and brutal force — that kills stone-wielding children in the name of public order — can put little distance between itself and the goons of South Africa.

And any nation that knowingly gives South Africa the military means with which to continue its suppression of its black majority puts at risk the support of millions of black Americans, many of whom want nothing more than for Israel to abandon both the tactics and its support of that racist nation.

Eric Sambo's death

WASHINGTON, Feb. 1, 1989

They say that Eric Sambo was tied to a tree for nearly two days and tortured to death by a man who openly admitted he committed the crime.

Sambo, a black South African laborer, was beaten savagely with a club because he unknowingly backed a tractor over a dog. The dead canine belonged to Sambo's employer, a white South African farmer, Jacobus Vorster, 23, who authorities charged with the murder.

But after considering all of the evidence and listening to the farmer's confession, a South African judge gave the killer a suspended sentence. Why?

Because, the judge ruled, Sambo was partly to blame for his own death since he failed to make sure the dog was not under the tractor before he started driving the vehicle.

Unbelievable?

The judge also had this to say: The convicted murderer would suffer "embarrassment" if made to go to jail because a report of his incarceration would be made available to government officials if he applied for a passport or gun permit.

Outrageous?

Well, the judge said his heart was in the right place. If he sent the farmer to jail, the white jurist explained, the other black laborers the man employed would have been left jobless.

In South Africa, the scales of justice, like everything else, are tilted heavily in favor of that nation's white minority.

If Sambo had been a Russian Jew, news of his death would have caused our State Department to convulse with diplomatic outrage. If he had been tied to a palm tree in Managua, Nicaragua, and savaged, Sambo would be the latest martyr of congressional conservatives.

But instead, Eric Sambo's death draws little notice in official Washington. Eight years after the Reagan administration told us that "constructive engagement" with — and not disengagement from — the madmen who govern South Africa would improve the plight of that nation's black majority, their political oppression and physical brutalization continues.

In his book *Future Shock*, Alvin Toffler talked about the numbing effect of rapidly occurring events.

In the world outside of South Africa's borders, the death of Sambo made little news. His murder was just the most recent in the daily slaughter of blacks in that pigmentocracy.

Back in 1960, people the world over cringed at reports that South African security forces fired on marchers in Sharpeville, killing 68 and wounding nearly 200.

Seventeen years later, it took the massacre of hundreds of black schoolchildren in Soweto to once again stoke the interest of the world media in the life-and-death struggles of blacks in South Africa.

Fire at will

Today, random acts of violence — ones in which blacks are brutalized by whites, and justice is savaged in the courts — no longer meet the definition of news for a world media numbed by the frequent occurrence of such events in South Africa.

Being tied to a tree and beaten to death over a two-day period for accidentally killing someone's pet dog is not the kind of story out of South Africa that makes the evening TV news in this country. Sambo's death got only fleeting coverage in U.S. newspapers.

But still, President Bush sticks to the "constructive engagement" policy of his predecessor. An abstraction that is blind to the surging body count, "constructive engagement" gives aid and comfort to Sambo's killer, and the judge who set him free.

South Africa craves the legitimacy that foreign recognition brings. And when such recognition challenges the international sanctions that seek to undermine that nation's apartheid government, it deflects the world's attention away from the human suffering that is a daily part of life for blacks in that racist nation.

What blacks in South Africa really need from the United States is not a foreign policy that panders to apartheid, but one that gives them the military means to bring it to an end.

Given the choice, I'm sure most blacks in South Africa would rather die waging war against apartheid than forfeit their lives to the senseless rage of a dog-loving farmer.

Lost innocence

WASHINGTON, Dec. 22, 1986

Fanie Goduka probably doesn't believe in Santa Claus anymore. He has long since lost the innocence of a child.

Accused last year of throwing stones at South African police, the 11-year-old black youth was held in a jail cell with adult prisoners for 57 days. During that time he was allegedly beaten by police and abused by his cellmates.

The youngster was denied bail four times because the magistrate believed he might "flee the country" if released. His mother was allowed to see him only twice during his imprisonment. Eventually acquitted of the charge, the boy still bears the scars of his experience. His mother says he often cries in his sleep and is afraid to leave his home for school or play.

Over the past two years, thousands of black children have been arrested and jailed, many without charges, by security forces in South Africa. Hundreds more have died at the hands of police.

Earlier this month, the South African government admitted it is holding about 300 black children in detention.

Government opponents, who say 8,000 black children have been detained since June, pleaded without success to have them released in time for Christmas.

Despite the conflicting accounts about the number of children jailed by the government under its state of emergency decree, one thing is certain: In South Africa's pigmentocracy, black children are at the forefront of the struggle to end apartheid.

This is so largely because most able-bodied adult opponents of South Africa's racial separation policies have been imprisoned, or have fled the country to join the resistance movement. The government's response to student-inspired protests, demonstrations and work boycotts has become more severe as increasing numbers of black youths take to the streets.

About one-third of all people detained by government forces since the beginning of the year have been black children, some as young as 8 years old — children who confront South African police with sticks and stones, and the courage of David.

"There is more official concern in this country about cruelty to animals than there is about cruelty to children," Sheena Duncan, a white anti-apartheid activist, complained recently.

As the number of black children detained increases, so too do reports of their torture and violation.

In August, a 12-year-old boy told reporters that while in jail he was tortured by police with electric shock that was applied to his hands, feet and genitals.

In another case, a 15-year-old girl was arrested by security forces and locked in a prison cell for several weeks with 12 men. She was moved only after questions about her treatment were raised by white opponents of South Africa's racist government.

Earlier this year, Bishop Desmond Tutu gave a public account of an encounter he had with a 15-year-old black youngster who had just been released from police custody.

"He spoke with great difficulty, as if his tongue was swollen and filled his mouth ... When he walked, it was a slow painful shuffle like a punch-drunk ex-boxer," Tutu said of the boy.

Like the madmen of Nazi Germany who were obsessed with their "master race" theory, the leaders of South Africa give no quarter to the children of those they seek to oppress.

In addition to the immediate harm that their abuse of black children renders, the South African government's actions inflict a greater injury. They imbue in the hearts and minds of yet another generation of that nation's black majority a hatred for South Africa's white minority that eventually may have devastating consequences.

"Increasing numbers of people, mainly young people, are becoming brutalized by the brutality they experience," a white anti-apartheid activist observed recently. And as a result, black children in South Africa — some as young as 8 years old — are learning the lessons of civil disobedience, rather than those offered in that nation's segregated schools.

They are learning to counter the violence of police with violence of their own. Adulthood is being forced upon them by a brutal system that makes no exceptions for children.

And young boys, like 11-year-old Fanie Goduka, are losing their innocence amid the stench and filth of a government jail cell.

Trauma victims

WASHINGTON, Nov. 5, 1986

Trauma victims often succumb to shock long before their physical injuries sap the life from them.

Leaders of South Africa's white-minority government have been traumatized for more than a decade by their fear of black-majority rule. Now, there are increasing signs that shock is setting in.

Late last month white and black moderates in Natal, one of South Africa's four provinces, approved a plan that would have given blacks unprecedented participation in the provincial government. The draft agreement came after eight months of negotiations among leaders of 35 groups — most of which represented the middle ground of South African politics.

Under the plan, Natal and the tribal homeland of KwaZulu would be merged and governed by a two-chamber provincial legislature. The dominant chamber of the legislature — the one that would choose Natal's prime minister — would consist of 100 members, selected in an election in which blacks and whites would participate equally.

Given that blacks would make up 85 percent of the reconstructed province, selection of a black prime minister was thought a certainty. Still, the plan fell short of creating a full-fledged isle of democracy within South Africa's pigmentocracy.

For instance, under the plan the smaller chamber of the provincial legislature would have 50 members, consisting of 10 representatives each from Natal's black, Afrikaans, English-speaking and Asian communities, plus 10 at-large members.

Passage of legislation would require approval of both chambers of parliament, and ultimately that of the country's national government. Also, whites in Natal would have veto authority over legislation affecting their "language, religion or culture," and a guarantee of at least three seats in the province's 10-member cabinet.

More a political sleight of hand than a real effort to bring about democratic rule in South Africa, the Natal plan offered the embattled nation a chance to distract some of the forces now working to topple the country's white-minority government.

But the ravages of shock often render one senseless.

Within hours after the power-sharing plan was adopted by moderate blacks and whites in Natal, it was rejected by South Africa's minister of home affairs, who said it had "unacceptable implications."

Wounded most seriously by the government's rejection of the Natal plan was Gatsha Buthelezi, the leading moderate among South Africa's blacks and chief of the nation's 6 million Zulus.

Buthelezi, who has drawn the ire of militant blacks in South Africa for his opposition to economic sanctions against the Pretoria government, had been one of the leading proponents of the Natal plan.

Rejection of the plan by government officials will almost certainly undermine Buthelezi's standing among South Africa's 25 million blacks, and the hopes of some of that nation's 6 million whites, that the

Zulu chief might calm the passions of an increasing number of blacks for majority rule.

One leading white opponent of South Africa's racist government said that the cabinet minister's rejection of the Natal plan represented "a reaction from bigots who have a death wish for South Africa."

But more likely, it was simply the mindless spasm of a traumatized government that is slipping deeper into shock. The symptoms abound.

While the home affairs minister was publicly attacking the Natal plan, the Afrikaans-led government of President P.W. Botha was acting to tighten the screws against those who oppose its apartheid policies.

Late last month, South African police were given the authority to ban indoor meetings of blacks thought to oppose government policies. Most large outdoor meetings have been banned for years.

And, caving in to government pressures, South African newspapers have agreed to a policy of "self-censorship" that extends beyond the government-imposed sanctions against reporting on the growing conflict between police and the country's oppressed black majority.

In announcing the newspapers' decision, Botha said the action was necessary because "South Africa is being subjected to a many-pronged but well coordinated revolutionary onslaught."

In truth, the fear of black rule causes leaders of the Pretoria government to hallucinate violently — to perceive dangers where none exist, and to respond with more and greater oppression of South Africa's black majority.

Weakened by their state of shock, the rulers of South Africa are slipping fast into a political coma.

Censored

WASHINGTON, Aug. 3, 1988

For the people who stick ratings on movies in this country, *Cry Freedom* poses less of a threat to movie-goers than *Revenge of the Nerds*.

But to the geeks who manage the internal security apparatus of South Africa's apartheid state, a marauding band of nerds on a college campus is a lot less threatening than the story of a friendship forged between a white newspaper editor and black activist in their pigmentocracy.

The gendarmes of apartheid

A few days ago South African police swooped down upon more than 30 movie theaters and confiscated copies of *Cry Freedom*, before all but a handful of movie-goers in that racially divided nation could see the anti-apartheid film. Maintenance of "public order" was offered as rationale for these seizures by the guardians of apartheid.

"The security forces are portrayed in such a negative light that their public image would be seriously undermined," South Africa's minister of information said, his words sounding more like a line out of the raunchy comedy, *Revenge of the Nerds*, than a rational explanation of his government's act of censorship.

In fact, the action taken by the South African government, which was designed to deny the nation's white minority an uncensored look at its brutal suppression of the country's black majority, could have passed as the latest sequel to the *Nerds* movie. As it is, the government's confiscation of *Cry Freedom* has shown once again the frailty of apartheid.

The movie is actually more the story of newspaper editor Donald Woods and the relationship he develops with black activist Steven Biko than an examination of the brutal tactics employed by South African security forces to oppress the nation's restive black majority. But to government security officials, any offering of truth about their dealings with black activists and the whites who befriend them is a threat to the kind of "public order" they seek to maintain.

For months, I had avoided seeing *Cry Freedom*, in an act of self-censorship. I just didn't want to submit my emotions to the immorality of South Africa's racist state, or the physical abuse its protectors visit upon those blacks who dare to resist apartheid. But when government officials in South Africa banned its viewing there, I felt compelled to see the movie here.

In the opening scene, security forces are shown raiding a settlement created by blacks in 1975 in violation of South African law. Their violent eviction of the black squatters, including the brutalization of women and children, was widely reported outside of South Africa at the time. But, as the movie depicts, South Africans were told that the razing of Crossroads was a peaceful event.

It was this conflict between the "official" version of events and that reported by the foreign media that led to the press censorship now in existence in South Africa. Throughout history, truth has been the archenemy of despots.

Fire at will

The movie offers viewers only a cursory look at the friendship that developed between Woods and Biko before the black activist's death in August 1977. It pays even less attention to the conflict between the report of security officers over the cause of Biko's death and the findings of an inquest that Woods helped to bring about.

For the record, South African police initially claimed Biko died as the result of a hunger strike. The inquest ruled that he succumbed to massive brain damage while in police custody — his badly bruised body having shown signs of sustained beatings.

And when Woods sought to tell the world of Biko's death, his passport was seized and he was banned — a form of internal exile, usually reserved for blacks, that severely restricts a person's contact with all but family members.

Much of the second half of the movie is devoted to the attempt by security officials to enforce the five-year banning order against Woods, and the newspaper editor's eventual escape from South Africa, the kind of story government officials would like to keep from the rest of that nation's white minority.

As a result of the censorship order, *Cry Freedom* will never be seen by most South Africans. But it's hard to imagine that such an act of desperation will long delay the collapse of South Africa's apartheid system — something for which both Steven Biko and Donald Woods sacrificed much.

CHAPTER 8
More than a canned sardine

"Not a single new idea has appeared in American journalism since the dawn of the Twentieth Century. It has become, like the law, a mere hugging of precedents, most of them of little dignity in either logic or fact."

— H. L. Mencken

AD he lived to see the day, H. L. Mencken surely would have delighted in the publication of USA TODAY. The man whose biting opinions were largely an irreverent attack on those who clung to precedent and power would have championed this "new idea" in American journalism.

Mencken detested those in the newspaper business who were slaves to tradition — people he often described as "Philistine," or worse. "There are not a dozen American newspapers of today with any more personality than so many sardines out of a can," he complained back in 1927.

It's hard to imagine that he would not have rejoiced in the new look that USA TODAY brings to journalism, if only because it dares to be so different.

Of course, in his support of USA TODAY, Mencken would have found himself at odds with many in our craft, just as he did throughout most of his newspaper career. Even now, 7 years after its founding, the paper continues to get more hard knocks than kudos from professional journalists.

I've got a good friend who delights in trashing USA TODAY, the flagship publication of Gannett. "It's the only paper I know of," he quips, "in which the lead and kicker to a story appear in the same paragraph."

Writing commentary for such a newspaper requires one to perfect the skills of a sprinter, rather than the endurance of a long-distance runner. The challenge is to be master of, rather than slave to, one's own ideas.

These columns, all of which appeared in USA TODAY, represent the best of my efforts to do both. ■

131

More than a canned sardine

Flags fit for burning

WASHINGTON, Feb. 16, 1989

Strike those colors. Burn the damn flags. It's time we declare the final victory. Like the symbols of Nazi Germany and imperial Japan, the flags of the old Confederacy ought to cause a violent churning in our national gut.

Instead, the Stars and Bars and the Confederate battle flag have become novelties of U.S. capitalism — just like the golden arches of McDonald's. They adorn pickup trucks, baseball caps, jackets and bumper stickers.

And, for reasons having to do more with self-flagellation than profit, several states have incorporated these rebellious images into their official flags.

In Montgomery, Ala., the Confederate battle flag of G.T. Beauregard — the general who ordered the attack on Fort Sumter, which started the Civil War — flies atop the state Capitol. A resolution to remove the secessionist flag is scheduled to be voted on next week by the Alabama Legislature.

Signs of the failed attempt by 11 Southern states to tear apart our nation — a conflict that killed more Americans than all our other wars combined — the flags of the Confederacy also stand for something else.

The Stars and Bars and the Confederate battle flag have become novelties of U.S. capitalism — just like the golden arches of McDonald's.

Anybody "who argues that the Confederate flag does not symbolize racism needs to have their heads examined," says Alvin Holmes, the Alabama state representative who introduced the resolution.

Like millions of other African-Americans, Holmes views the Confederate flags as constant reminders that slavery was a central issue in the Civil War.

The flag that flies atop the Alabama Capitol was ordered there in 1963 in defiance of the civil rights movement, which began just a few blocks away. Only the shameful dunderheads of the Ku Klux Klan give this defeated flag more prominence.

For many Southerners, the Civil War is "what A.D. is elsewhere; they date from it," writer and social commentator Mark Twain is quoted as having said.

And for far too many Southerners, the Confederate flags signal their refusal to accept today what Robert E. Lee came to understand at Appomattox Court House 124 years ago: The South lost the war.

So tear down those traitorous flags!

The final solution

WASHINGTON, Feb. 14, 1989

It was, after all, just a call for some "modest changes."

That's the way Chief Justice William Rehnquist put it last week when he called for reform of the process by which people on death row are allowed to appeal their sentences.

Troubled by the delays states experience in carrying out death penalties, the chief justice wants to tinker a bit with the habeas corpus system that allows for multiple review of a judge's execution order.

The last time the writ of habeas corpus was so savaged, Abraham Lincoln arrested the grandson of Francis Scott Key in Baltimore and locked him up in Fort McHenry — without ever charging him with a crime, or taking the case to trial.

As with Rehnquist's suggestion, Lincoln's action seemed more politically expedient than legally correct.

Hurrying up the process by which those convicted of capital crimes are put to death might reduce the legal system's paperwork burden and please those angered by Ted Bundy's nine-year stay on death row, but the mere idea ought to send a chill up the spines of right-thinking people.

Any legal scheme that seeks to shortcut the appeals process risks rushing innocent people — and those undeserving of such severe punishment — to their end.

According to the NAACP Legal Defense Fund, there are 2,180 persons awaiting execution in this country. And while 106 persons have been executed since 1973, more than 1,400 individuals on death row had their sentences reversed, largely as a result of the appeals process.

Given the bad legal representation poor defendants often get, it sometimes requires several appeals — and a new attorney — before the proper legal arguments are presented to overturn a faulty conviction.

What Rehnquist actually wants is unclear. How he would cut the appeals process was not fully stated. But there should be little doubt that what he seems to be offering is a kind of "McJustice" — a fast-food approach to jurisprudence that would likely give the U.S. legal system painful indigestion.

"Modest changes," indeed!

Back in 1729, Jonathan Swift offered the people of England something he called "A Modest Proposal" to reduce the country's burgeoning population of illegitimate children. They "should be offered for sale to persons of quality" for consumption, he said.

And properly skinned, Swift added, their carcasses could be used to make "admirable gloves for ladies, and summer boots for fine gentlemen." Fortunately for England's children, everyone recognized that Swift's satire was no serious call to action.

Given the unnecessary human carnage Rehnquist's idea would bring if adopted, many people must be wondering now if the chief justice was speaking as a jurist — or a satirist — when he proposed his "modest changes."

When history insults

WASHINGTON, Feb. 1, 1989

The problem with Black History Month is it comes just once a year.

For the 28 days of February, people across this nation will pander to the contemptuous notion that — like Groundhog Day — the history of African-Americans is a novelty of the Gregorian calendar.

Schoolteachers will pull out dusty pictures of Nat Love, revive the memory of Harriet Tubman and extol the virtues of Frederick Douglass and Booker T. Washington. Politicians will genuflect uncontrollably at the mention of Martin Luther King Jr. And television stations across the USA will offer viewers a steady diet of Black History Month programming, including reruns of *Shaft* and *Cleopatra Jones*.

Let's face it; this is not what Carter G. Woodson had in mind when, in 1926, he launched Negro History Week.

What he wanted was to draw attention to the contributions of African-Americans to U.S. history — to convince other Americans that we, too, played a significant role in the building of this country. What has resulted is something far less profound.

It now seems that only in February does this nation awaken to the reality that it took more than a few wagon trains of white men and women to tame the West. For many, it is only during this 28-day period that they openly concede African-Americans are responsible for a good bit of the culture and technology that transformed a once backwoods nation into a world power.

More than anything else, Black History Month is the reprieve we give to textbook publishers and curriculum writers, most of whom are guilty of treating what goes on in February as little more than a footnote in the materials they produce for our schools. For educators, it is more expedient than the massive overhaul of curricula that is needed to mainstream the teaching of the contributions of African-Americans to this nation.

Come March, what our children are taught in February is largely shelved, exchanged for more "traditional" history lessons. Doting public officials move on to the next politically expedient observance, and millions of uncertain schoolchildren are left to ponder the meaning of it all.

I say let's take a revolutionary step: Starting next month, let's insist that the history of African-Americans be required learning in schools, whenever classes are in session.

The time has come to give people in this country what Woodson really wanted — the uncensored version of American history, year-round.

Let's end the insulting nonsense of Black History Month.

A continental divide

WASHINGTON, Sept. 13, 1988

Damn those guys Lewis and Clark!

Ever since Meriwether Lewis and William Clark stumbled their way

More than a canned sardine

to the Pacific shore, people with the good sense not to invest in real estate west of the Rockies have had to pander to those who moved across that "great divide."

Remember the transcontinental railroad? The pony express? How about Utah and Nevada? All were created for a single purpose: to link the West Coast to the rest of the USA.

And how did those Western ingrates repay us? They stole just about everything this side of Denver that wasn't bolted to the Brooklyn Bridge.

First, they took the movie industry from New Jersey. Then they swiped the baseball Dodgers and Giants from New York. The *Merv Griffin Show* from Philadelphia. Motown records from Detroit. And last year, they snatched the football Cardinals from St. Louis.

We Easterners have put up with all this abuse — and the "out-of-body experiences" Westerners credit for their brazen behavior — for far too long. The time has come to stand up to these sun-drenched looters.

I say we draw the line at Monday night football. For 18 years, those of us who watch the game on the East Coast have had to suffer through after-midnight finishes and early-morning fatigue so West Coast fans could see the contest "live" right after the evening news.

Now that ABC has pushed the game time forward from 9 p.m. to 8 p.m. EDT — for September only — while the network is in head-to-head competition with the Olympics on NBC, football fans from Phoenix to Portland are whining in their sushi and guacamole. Why? Because for just four weeks they must rush home from work in time for the 5 p.m. kickoffs. Give me a break!

Talk about inconvenience. Every time the Orioles play on the West Coast, I have to put in for a 10:30 p.m. wake-up call just to see the first pitch.

If West Coast football fans are looking for relief, I've got the answer. Return the Dodgers to Brooklyn and Motown to Detroit. Give the Lakers back to Minneapolis.

Agree to all this and they can have Monday night football at any time of their choosing. And there's this bonus: History might treat more kindly the memory of Lewis and Clark.

One turkey of an idea

WASHINGTON, Aug. 8, 1988

"This bird simply won't fly."

That's the advice close advisers should have given George Bush when Dan Quayle's name was first mentioned as a running mate for the Republican presidential candidate.

Forget Quayle's decision in 1969 to safeguard the borders of Indiana through membership in the National Guard rather than risk being drafted to service in Vietnam. Disregard his unremarkable grades at DePauw University and the pleading he had to do to win admission to Indiana University law school after his application was rejected.

Assume that Bush knew nothing of this "baggage" Quayle brings to the Republican ticket and just consider the "positives" the Indiana senator's presence on the GOP slate is supposed to represent.

Quayle, Republican image makers say, is a good complement to the Bush ticket. He's handsome. Conservative. And at 41, a member of that largely amorphous group we have come to call "baby boomers." All characteristics thought to be attractive to voters not otherwise drawn to the Bush campaign in sufficient numbers.

The guys who sold Bush this bill of goods are probably the same fellas who convinced dodo birds that their species would survive a lot longer if they shortened their wings and quit flying.

The only constituency Dan Quayle is sure to appeal to are the ultra-conservatives within the Republican Party — a political bloc that has already locked itself in to the GOP.

What George Bush needs to win in November are the swing votes of the so-called Reagan Democrats.

Winning them over will require more than the help of a pretty face and a "yuppie" label. Yuppies tend to be more moderate than both Bush and Quayle on issues like abortion and defense spending. And, largely working class, they will find it hard to relate to a Republican ticket made up of wealthy patricians.

For balance, Bush would have fared a lot better with Sen. Robert Dole of Kansas or Gov. Thomas Kean of New Jersey as his running mate. As it is, he appears stuck with J. Danforth Quayle III, a choice that is turning out to be quite a turkey.

137

More than a canned sardine

A national obsession

WASHINGTON, July 21, 1989
It's the fourth quarter of the football game, with just seconds to go. The score is tied. The ball is on the 12-yard line.

Does the coach send in his field-goal kicker and go for the three-point victory? Or, does he try to score a touchdown and beat the five-point betting spread?

Any football fan with an IQ over 80 knows the answer. He takes the more certain scoring opportunity and goes for the field goal.

And come fall, when thousands of people plop down their hard-earned cash with the Oregon state lottery for a chance to bet legally on NFL games, the answer to this question won't change. The coach will still go for the field goal.

So why all the fuss over Oregon's plan to make legal what so many of us do now — bet on football games?

With millions of dollars changing hands in illegal sports betting, including those "harmless" office pools, it comes as no surprise that a state lottery has muscled in on the action.

Sure, lotteries are this nation's newest form of regressive taxation; but, without them, balancing many state budgets would be a greater gamble.

All taxing schemes feed on themselves. To keep up with the pace of government spending and inflation, tax collectors are pressed to increase revenues — and that includes those who run lotteries in 28 states and the District of Columbia. They are under constant pressure to come up with new games to keep people betting.

If that offends you, try getting voters in those states to approve new taxes to replace revenue that would be lost if those lotteries were shut down.

Already, betting on sporting events is legal in Nevada. Still, the NFL is threatening to sue Oregon over its decision. Anybody want to bet on the outcome?

Listen: Gambling, like crack cocaine, has become a national obsession. Atlantic City, Reno, Lake Tahoe and Las Vegas are just the tip of the iceberg. From the bingo parlors of Salinas, Calif., to the poker tables of Deadwood, S.D., gambling revenues are funding local governments.

Voters in Iowa have already approved riverboat gambling, to begin in 1991. Illinois is thinking about following suit. So what makes football a sacred cow?

Since it seems we are stuck with legalized gambling, consider this: Given the choice, which would you rather do? Risk two bucks on the random selection of a lottery computer or bet it on the outcome of a game most sports fans think they understand?

Quitting time

WASHINGTON, May 5, 1989

Yesterday, Jim Wright got the public hearing he's desperately been seeking. Today, he should step down as House speaker.

Before the televised hearing, most people in this country knew nothing of Wright or his alleged misdeeds. Today, his recognition factor is up sharply, but his political stock is on the skids. Worse yet, the Texas Democrat is dragging his party down with him. Accused of 69 violations of congressional ethics rules, Wright is hopelessly mired in a political cesspool that threatens to leave its stench on his Democratic colleagues long after he leaves the political stage.

As his lawyers went before the House ethics committee in an attempt to reduce the charges of ethical wrongdoing down to a manageable number, Wright was stung by new reports of questionable financial activities. For the speaker — who is but two heartbeats away from the presidency — the time has come to put the interests of party ahead of principle. Chances of a protracted public fight to defend himself are driven more by personal pride than political instincts.

Saying they had "reason to believe" he acted improperly, the ethics committee members last month voted unanimously to cite the speaker for a long list of violations. Should Wright take his fight to the trial stage, this same 12-member group — evenly divided between Democrats and Republicans — will sit in judgment of his guilt or innocence. The full House, and its Democratic majority, would have the final say as to his punishment if he is found guilty.

Forcing his Democratic colleagues to run this political gauntlet would squander whatever chances House Democrats had of putting their imprint on the policies of George Bush during the early months of his presidency. Worse yet, a drawn-out public hearing on Wright's alleged ethics violations would imperil the re-election bids of some House Democrats and impede the party's ability to put together a winning strategy for the 1992 presidential election.

Of course, much of this damage can be avoided. Jim Wright should quit his post as House speaker and move quickly to Congress' back bench.

Closing the gap

WASHINGTON, Nov. 16, 1988

If George Bush received a mandate in last week's presidential election, it is this: Bring us closer together.

In winning the presidency, Bush was the overwhelming choice of white Protestants and Southern conservatives. But a majority of women and just about every black who went to the polls voted for his opponent, Michael Dukakis.

The USA Bush inherits is one in which racial and sexual polarization have taken on a greater sophistication. The Klansmen and chauvinists of past decades largely have given way to those who cloak their biases in political ideology.

President Bush must find a way to bridge the gap between his overwhelmingly white, male support base and the hopes of those who voted against him that they, too, will get a slice of the American dream.

I'm not talking about the creation of a one-party state or a political utopia that would be the scourge of political operative Lee Atwater, but rather the creation of a climate that would usher in a much-needed change in this nation's political landscape. And the time to begin is now!

Over the next several weeks, the president-elect will oversee a transition in which thousands of Ronald Reagan's political appointees are replaced by those selected by Bush and his advisers. For many, it is a Thanksgiving that only comes with the changing of a presidential administration.

If Bush listens to his jubilant troops, he will use simple criteria to garrison these jobs: support of his campaign and loyalty to the conservative ideology that dominated his run for the White House.

But if, as he said the day after his victory, Bush wants to be the president of all Americans, he should beware of such a strategy. In the words of Democratic convention keynoter Ann Richards, "that old dog won't hunt."

To broaden his support base — and potentially the Republican Party — Bush has got to be more "inclusive."

Sure, he should dole out the plums to supporters; they deserve some rewards. But if Bush wants to pull women and blacks into the GOP, he needs to find some important places for them in his administration, too.

With thousands of political jobs up for grabs, George Bush has a lot of patronage to spread around. Using some of these positions to expand his constituency is more than good politics. It's the kind of action from which true mandates spring.

Maternal justice

WASHINGTON, May 17, 1989

Jailing mothers who expose their unborn babies to illegal drugs may satisfy our sense of justice, but it will do nothing to end this nation's drug epidemic.

When Melanie Green's baby died earlier this year in Rockford, Ill., an outraged prosecutor charged her with manslaughter and supplying drugs to a minor in the cocaine-induced death of her 2-day-old daughter.

The cocaine, which Green is believed to have taken during her pregnancy, apparently found its way into the unborn baby's bloodstream. The result was fatal.

Outraged? You're damn right I am. But if we're going to win this drug war, we must be driven by something a lot more rational than a quest for blind revenge.

Throwing Melanie Green into jail is not the answer.

Prosecutors might earn badly needed Brownie points with a public fed up with the drug trade that is savaging so many of our neighborhoods, but there is no real victory to be found in locking up junkies — people more in need of therapy than incarceration.

More than a canned sardine

Besides, clogging our legal system with drug addicts would leave little space for those who traffic in the deadly poisons. Better we offer addicts the clinical and psychological help they need to break their drug dependency.

Experts say there are 375,000 babies born each year to drug-abusing mothers. Going after them is tantamount to trying to stop an advancing army with a lone sniper.

Our goal should be to do all we can to save at-risk babies by drawing their mothers into the prenatal medical programs that many of them now forgo.

Putting these women in jail would have just one predictable result: an increase in the need for foster-care parents, another national problem of crisis proportion.

I say we marshal our forces for a frontal attack on those who profit from the sale of cocaine and other illegal drugs. If we are truly intent on waging war against the illegal-drug trade, let's go after the traders. Putting these lowlifes behind bars is a winning strategy.

Trotting the sorry figure of Melanie Green before a judge and jury is not.

Who decides?

WASHINGTON, March 3, 1989

They say that nature abhors a vacuum. And so, too, it seems, do television viewers.

While the miracles of life are credited to Mother Nature, the wonders of television programming are thought to have no such doting parent.

When crusaders of the ideological right take networks to task for programs they think offensive, their protests echo in the vacuum that has been created by deregulation and congressional neglect of the broadcast industry.

The so-called "New Puritans" may be a bit too prudish when it comes to television programming, but their point is well taken. Someone besides the small clique of network executives who pass on most of what we see on TV ought to have a say about the images that are broadcast into our homes.

Given the choice between the whiz kids of network programming and industry pressure groups — such as Viewers for Quality Television — the activists seem to be the lesser of two evils. When it comes to shows like *Designing Women* and *Frank's Place,* which was canceled last year, the groups — which favored those shows — have proven better judges of viewer interests.

In my house there are seven TVs — three of which my wife, Wanda, uses in combination with VCRs to keep up with everything from the daytime soaps to *Falcon Crest* and *Knots Landing.* She records the shows for later viewing.

But in recent months, I've noticed that while she's still recording the same programs, my wife spends less time watching them.

Increasingly, she uses the fast-forward button on the remote control to rush by programs or scenes she considers "silly." Like the New Puritans, she, too, has become a TV censor.

And like other critics of the network programming schedule, she has only two options: watch, or turn them off. Hardly the kind of choices that threaten to expand the networks' shrinking audiences.

Last year, my mailbox filled with letters from irate viewers when CBS — in an act of obvious self-flagellation — dropped *Frank's Place.* But the complaints that came to me and the network did little to jerk CBS out of its stupor.

To prevent those on the tundra of public opinion from making programming decisions, network executives have to be more responsive to the rest of us.

And they can begin by bringing back *Frank's Place.*

A smoky death

WASHINGTON, June 23, 1989

I support a person's right to smoke. If people want to regularly light up cigarettes and douse their bodies in the smoke and carcinogens they emit, who am I to deny them such kinky pleasures?

But when it comes to forcing me and other non-smokers to share their death wish, that's where I draw the line. There are many things in life we all must learn to tolerate. Most are mere annoyances. Some —

like Morton Downey Jr. and people who talk through an entire movie while seated in front of me — rate a bit higher on the scale of things that really turn me off.

No non-smoker should be made to suffer the presence of a lighted cigarette and the deadly smoke it spews forth, in a closed space. Those addicted to this slow death have no rights that require non-smokers to be subjected to this abuse.

That's the message members of Congress are getting as they consider an extension of the federal ban against smoking on airline flights of less than two hours.

It's bad enough that smokers play Russian roulette with their own lives every time they inhale, but according to a soon-to-be-released Environmental Protection Agency study, their nasty habit also has a health-threatening impact on others in buildings where they smoke. The report finds that non-smokers in closed areas with smokers cannot avoid the ill effects of cigarettes.

If nicotine junkies must have a regular fix of tobacco, they should be required to head for the open spaces of a parking lot or city street. Forcing them outdoors only begs the question, but such a move gives the rest of us time to clear our lungs while we contemplate how the greenhouse effect and cigarette smoke might eventually combine to suffocate the entire planet.

Given the EPA's findings, Congress should not only extend the current ban, it should ban smoking altogether on commercial aircraft and other forms of public transportation. Being crammed into an airplane or train with a smoker is more than a simple annoyance. It's a life-threatening situation that we should all desperately try to avoid.

A sobering idea

WASHINGTON, June 2, 1989

If moderation is good for drinkers, why shouldn't it be practiced by advertisers?

Getting people to cut back on the booze they consume, particularly when they do their drinking in public places, has become something of a national pastime in recent years.

Some jurisdictions have gone so far as to threaten bartenders with prosecution for selling one too many drinks to a customer. Several professional baseball teams have limited the times during a game when beer is sold to fans in the stands.

And many local governments — concerned about the abuse of alcoholic beverages by teen-agers — have enacted "keg laws" that penalize parents for the drunken behavior of their children.

All this in the name of moderation.

And now Surgeon General C. Everett Koop says the time has come for the companies that produce intoxicating drinks to rein themselves in. Why not?

By voluntarily restricting the amount of advertising they do in situations where their audience is likely to consist of large numbers of young people, these firms can help solve one of our most troubling public health problems.

Alcohol-related accidents killed more people in this country last year than did AIDS. One in five deaths among people ages 15 to 20 involves alcohol.

Reducing the consumption of booze among young drinkers could save thousands of lives a year. And while keeping these young people alive is, understandably, Koop's primary concern, their long-term survival also is in the interest of the liquor industry. A moderate drinker who lives to a ripe old age will likely spend a lot more money on alcoholic beverages than a heavy drinker who goes to an early grave.

If it's so important to solve the "tastes great, less filling" dispute, why not do it with point-of-sale advertising in bars and liquor stores, rather than with 30-second commercials during the Super Bowl?

And, one last point. If Spuds MacKenzie is really such a great party animal, why doesn't he put down that beer and get out on the dance floor?

The chance of a lifetime

WASHINGTON, April 26, 1989

I saw him as soon as I guided my car onto Interstate 83.

The man in the aging Datsun gave me a quick glance and then

floored his gas pedal. No doubt about it, he was after my money. Our two cars sped north, racing toward Pennsylvania and a shot at the Keystone State's $100 million lottery.

Despite the many thousands of people who have combined to inflate the odds against winning today's bloated jackpot, I knew I had but one person to beat for this king's ransom — some guy in an old Datsun.

I wouldn't cross the street to buy a ticket for a measly $2 million lottery prize, but for $100 million I was willing to race this guy to a Pennsylvania lottery machine and a chance to win the kind of cash that puts you on speaking terms with Malcolm Forbes and Bunker Hunt.

Forty-five miles ahead was a one-way ticket to the good life, and the only person between me and this wealth was now racing his car ahead of mine.

Chasing after a lottery jackpot nearly the size of Grenada's gross national product is a gamble worth taking. For the $1 price of a ticket, a single winner could join the ranks of the filthy rich.

Think about it. A dream house and the red BMW convertible my wife has been craving. Month-long vacations in Tahiti and Martinique. And, of course, a visit from Robin Leach.

People who win $2 million, $4 million or $6 million in a state lottery get just enough money to whet their appetite for a lifestyle they can ill afford. But the winner of $100 million is nothing short of a real plutocrat.

I pressed my foot on the gas, and my car surged past the Datsun. I beat its driver to a Pennsylvania lottery machine by at least 90 seconds.

Returning to my car with a handful of tickets, I saw the beaten man standing in line. On his face was the look of someone who could never enjoy the wealth I am about to experience.

$100 million would ruin him. He's the kind of guy who would be a lot happier to win just a million or two.

The court strikes out

WASHINGTON, June 8, 1989

It's got to make you wonder: Does Supreme Court Justice Byron White understand the difference between Cito Gaston, the Toronto Blue Jays' new manager, and Billy Martin, the man who's had more second chances in baseball than Elizabeth Taylor did in marriage?

Gaston, just the fourth black manager in major league history, was forced to languish for weeks in the job on an interim basis while team officials pursued several whites for the position. Not until they exhausted their search for a white manager did Blue Jays' officials relent and give Gaston the permanent assignment.

Given the high court's ruling Monday shifting the burden of proof in employment-discrimination cases from employers to their workers, the Supreme Court would find nothing wrong with this turn of events.

Without specific evidence of discrimination, White and his court colleagues would contend, the virtual absence of minorities from baseball and football management is an acceptable employment practice.

Al Campanis, rejoice. Bring back Jimmy "The Greek" Snyder. Baseball and football, sports dominated by black and Hispanic athletes, can continue to ignore qualified minorities for management jobs on the field and in the executive suites.

The mere coincidence of their exclusion from senior management jobs in these sports is no proof of racial bias, the court's conservative majority has concluded. I'm unconvinced.

In life — if not in law — common sense suggests if blacks and other minorities are talented enough to lead football and baseball teams to victory on the field, some of them must possess the necessary skills to manage a team's success from the sidelines.

Only two of the 26 big-league baseball teams have black managers. Both got the job while their teams were in last place — an employment practice in itself that ought to be considered a deliberate act of discrimination.

Also, not a single National Football League team has had a black head coach.

To the court, these would be mere statistical disparities. But to a good number of former professional football and baseball players, they constitute a troubling reality.

Room for all

WASHINGTON, March 2, 1989

All around the nation, "adults only" signs are coming down from housing complexes that used to lock out families with children. Good riddance!

Beginning this month, the protection of the federal Fair Housing Act is being extended to outlaw a form of discrimination that has allowed three-quarters of all rental units to limit access to families with children.

Twenty-five percent of these units were closed totally to children. Such a policy of denying shelter to parents with children was rightfully viewed by Congress as an objectionable practice — one that rivals some states' welfare rules for its disruptive impact on the family.

Like those sections of the Fair Housing Act intended to end racial discrimination in the sale and rental of housing, the bar against "adults only" housing units does away with one more form of senseless bias.

Yes, people without children have rights, too. But they are hard-pressed to argue convincingly that their housing rights should extend beyond the home or apartment they live in. They have no more right to set age limits on who lives next door than they do to dictate the race of their neighbors.

As a concession to our senior citizens — most of whom have survived countless hours of exposure to this nation's children — the new law permits these exceptions to the "adults only" ban: Exclusions are granted to facilities in which every resident is over 62 or 80 percent of the occupants are at least 55.

"Civil rights laws represent an effort to balance the rights of people to be left alone with the rights of people to be protected from discrimination," says Lisa Mihaly of the Children's Defense Fund. The elimination of "adults only" housing is not a race or class issue, she says. "It's a family issue."

And for those whining adults who are fearful of children moving in next door, there is this: Nothing in the new law prevents landlords from denying housing to families whose children are unruly and destructive.

For that matter, landlords appear also to be free to give the boot to adults who are guilty of similar behavior. After all, fair is fair.

CHAPTER 9
I wonder as I wander

AS I traveled about the country, many things caught my attention and stuck in my craw — questions that have gone unanswered by others, largely for lack of interest. But for me they cause a raising of the brow.

The following columns represent a collection of afterthoughts — bits and pieces of my thinking — that piled up over a period of time.

Arsenio Hall, the comedian turned late-night talk show host, knows what I'm talking about. On his show he does an occasional skit about "things that make you go hmmm."

Like Hall, I often encounter things that cause me to pause. Some examples:

Why did Major League Baseball need to hire someone to help find minority ex-players who are interested in a management job in the sport? If the teams found these guys once, why do they need help locating them again? Hmmm.

How much of a choice did the voters of Philadelphia really have when they last voted for mayor in the "City of Brotherly Love?" The candidates were Democrat Wilson Goode and Republican Frank Rizzo.

Goode, the city's first black mayor, once ordered police to drop a bomb on a house in which radicals were holed up. The resulting fire gutted 61 homes and left 250 people homeless.

Rizzo, a white conservative and former Democratic mayor, used the racial fears of whites in Philadelphia to maintain his control of City Hall.

Given their records of public service, why would anyone want to give either a second chance? Hmmm.

OK, so the questions raised in this chapter are not earthshaking. But they were troubling enough to catch my attention — questions that made me wonder as I wandered. ∎

The issue of trash

WASHINGTON, Oct. 19, 1987

I wonder as I wander. Footnotes on life from a black perspective.

Does it come as a surprise to anyone that the top issue in Philadelphia's mayoral race is trash?

That was obvious to me when incumbent Mayor W. Wilson Goode and former Mayor Frank Rizzo, respectively, won the Democratic and Republican primaries earlier this year.

Both men say they have plans to dispose of the city's garbage — the solid-waste variety that is. But as the candidates wrestle with Philadelphia's mounting trash disposal problem, no relief is in sight for city voters. Next month either Rizzo or Goode will win election to City Hall, which means that it will take at least four more years to solve all of Philadelphia's trash removal problems.

■

Has anyone taken a serious look at the questionnaire baseball's newest "super scout" is sending out to minority former players?

The document being circulated by Harry Edwards, the black sociologist hired by Major League Baseball to find black and Hispanic former players for management positions, asks for, among other things: the number, sex and age of their children; and such vital information as the occupation and education of their parents.

Both men say they have plans to dispose of the city's garbage — the solid-waste variety that is.

What does any of this have to do with selecting a black baseball manager, or a Hispanic general manager? Nothing, of course. But then what does Harry Edwards really have to do with the hiring of minorities in baseball front-office and field-management jobs? That's right, nothing.

■

Fire at will

How did John Connally, former U.S. treasury secretary and Texas governor, get $93 million in debt to financial institutions with only $13 million in assets?

Most black entrepreneurs in the Lone Star State can't borrow a dime more than the collateral they produce, and even then many banks are reluctant to do the deal. Now that's a Texas-size double standard.

∎

Has Albert Gore emerged as the "Great White Hope" Democrats have been looking for to stave off a Jesse Jackson romp of next year's Super South presidential primary?

Party leaders certainly hope so. They have tried mightily to find someone to challenge Jackson's lead in the 14 Southern states that will hold primaries on March 8. A Jackson victory in the South, at a time when Democrats are trying to shake their liberal image in an effort to win back the support of white voters, is their worst nightmare.

But Gore is not likely to derail the Jackson "Southern Express." His low name-recognition, combined with the presence of other relatively strong white candidates in the race, will keep Jackson ahead of the pack.

When the votes are counted in the March 8 primaries, Jesse Jackson will emerge as the biggest delegate winner, and Albert Gore's presidential bid will be lost. Enter Massachusetts Gov. Michael Dukakis.

∎

Can I say enough about my disdain for the role into which baseball super scout Harry Edwards has been cast?

Probably not.

Have you heard this sociology-professor-turned-recruiter's latest brainstorm for finding minorities for major league baseball management jobs?

Next month he will hold no less than three regional conventions to match minority candidates with baseball management types — in other words, a jobs fair. What a novel idea.

This thing has gone beyond simply being a bad idea, to being downright silly. All baseball executives need do to find black and Hispanic former players is to check the addresses on the pension and deferred-salary checks baseball sends to these men.

If team owners are serious about getting more minorities into management positions, they should begin by hiring Reggie Jackson — a no-

nonsense former player — to oversee the implementation of their commitment.

And what about Harry Edwards? Maybe he can help this country's newspapers solve their minority employment problems. Does anybody know what Carl Rowan's mother did for a living?

■

Is anybody really surprised by this bit of news?

The Census Bureau reported last month that black-owned businesses are more likely to hire black workers than are firms owned by whites. Nearly 70 percent of black companies have black employees, while only 40 percent of white businesses in this country employ blacks.

For most blacks that's not news, it's history.

Evacuate Philadelphia

WASHINGTON, Aug. 16, 1987

I wonder as I wander. Footnotes on life from a black perspective.

When does the evacuation of Philadelphia begin? Now that the candidates for mayor in that city have been whittled down to incumbent W. Wilson Goode and former Mayor Frank Rizzo, people in Philadelphia ought to be heading for the exits.

Goode, you recall, is the mayor who ordered the bombing of a rowhouse in a botched attempt to oust members of a radical group called MOVE. The bomb set off a blaze that gutted 61 houses and left 250 people homeless. Eleven MOVE members were killed in the inferno.

Rizzo, the law-and-order cop turned politician whose relationship with Philadelphia blacks caused racial polarization to rise to new heights during his administration, ran the city like a Gestapo colonel.

Now that it is certain one of these two men will have their soiled hands on Philadelphia's power throttle for the next four years, the city should be declared a federal disaster area. At the very least, civil defense officials ought to be checking their contingency plans.

■

Talk about religious charismatics. Why doesn't the Rev. Jerry Falwell offer to turn the PTL ministry over to the Reverend Ike, the flashy black televangelist?

By doing so, he can prove to his detractors that he is not bent upon getting a corner on the televangelism market, in much the same way that the brothers Hunt once tried to hoard silver.

And, such an action would put Falwell at the forefront of an effort to desegregate one of the nation's most racially polarized institutions — the church.

■

If Jesse Jackson is the front-runner for the Democratic Party's presidential nomination, then what has happened to his media coverage?

When Gary Hart led the pack, he could not make a speech or other public appearance without attracting the attention of dozens of journalists.

Now that Jackson is out front in the national polls, it seems that political reporters and their editors have taken a siesta. Too bad.

■

How many of you believe Atlanta Mayor Andrew Young when he said he was just offering "pastoral counseling" when he called the wife of former state Sen. Julian Bond shortly before she was to meet with the FBI?

To refresh your memory, Bond's wife had accused her husband and Mayor Young of snorting cocaine. She told Atlanta police her husband used the illegal drug every two hours. Bond's wife recanted her charges after receiving the telephone call from Young, who is also a Baptist minister.

And there are still those who question the power of prayer.

■

Have the playing fields of professional sports become the new civil rights battleground?

Look for black activists to use the civil rights tactics of the '60s — picketing, boycotts and sit-ins — in an attempt to bring about equality of opportunity in the sports arena.

But don't expect to see major changes until black athletes join in the protest. If they walk out on professional sports, hockey will become the new national pastime, or worse tennis — and the owners of professional baseball, basketball and football teams will begin to feel a serious financial pinch.

■

Who does Isiah Thomas think he is defiling one of professional basketball's sacred cows?

If you didn't hear, Thomas, a black player with the Detroit Pistons, had the audacity to suggest that Larry Bird, pro basketball's "Great White Hope," is a media creation.

"He's a very, very good" player, Thomas said of Bird. "But if he were black, he'd be just one of many good players" in the NBA, Thomas complained. Obviously the former Indiana University star doesn't understand the difference between black and white athletes.

Larry Bird uses intelligence, smarts and something called "court generalship" to propel the Boston Celtics to the top ranks of professional basketball every year. Black players, like Magic Johnson and Thomas, lead their teams to victory using their primal skills.

You think I'm kidding? Don't take my word for it. Just ask almost any sportscaster or reporter.

■

Finally, why is everyone so upset over the statement made by Supreme Court Justice Thurgood Marshall, who said the Constitution was "flawed from the start"?

Marshall cited the Founding Fathers' failure to protect the rights of women and blacks when they framed the Constitution 200 years ago.

Surely this nation is ready to agree this failure is a black mark on its white record. Right?

A matter of debate

WASHINGTON, Sept. 28, 1988

I wonder as I wander. Footnotes on life from a black perspective.

Why is it that Baltimore Mayor Kurt Schmoke can make grown men holler when he simply calls for a debate, but George Bush and Michael Dukakis generate only a few whimpers when they engage in one?

Could it be that Schmoke's call for a national debate on the question of decriminalizing such drugs as cocaine and heroin is a lot more interesting to most of us than listening to Bush and Dukakis talk for 90 minutes on most other subjects?

Fire at will

■

Does anyone besides me think it a bit unfair that an athlete who is caught using drugs for the first time is treated more harshly than one who is a three-time loser?

Olympic sprinter Ben Johnson, who was found with traces of an anabolic steroid in his body after winning the 100-meter dash in Seoul, now faces a two-year suspension from international track competition.

But New York Giants linebacker Lawrence Taylor, who has failed three drug tests, is now scheduled to return to play with the professional football team after serving just a 30-day suspension.

Taylor's brief trip to the woodshed for his third offense will cost him roughly $250,000 of the $1 million he was scheduled to earn this year. For his first offense, Johnson is expected to forfeit millions of dollars in future earnings.

■

What ever happened to Harry Edwards, the black sociologist and part-time radical, who was hired by Major League Baseball to help club owners find minorities for front-office and field-management jobs?

To the best of my knowledge, the only person he can take personal credit for finding a job is Al Campanis, the former Los Angeles Dodgers official who was bounced by the team when he went on national TV and suggested that blacks lacked the right stuff to hold management jobs in the sport. Edwards hired Campanis to help him do his job — which is probably why we haven't heard much from Harry Edwards since.

■

How many massacres and human rights violations must Haiti produce before the United States props up a Contra-like band to fight for democracy in that Caribbean nation?

Or is it the case that as long as Haitian dictators cater to Reagan's fear of communism, they will remain free to brutalize the people of this hemisphere's first independent black nation?

■

What role has Jesse Jackson been asked to play in the presidential campaign by Michael Dukakis, the Democratic Party nominee?

For weeks following the Democratic convention, close friends of Jackson could be heard complaining that the runner-up for the party's

presidential nomination was being shunned by Dukakis campaign officials. And while some of his top supporters recently have been named
to the Dukakis staff, Jackson himself has not been very visible on the
campaign trail.

Do you think Dukakis has figured out how to win in November
without Jackson's strong support?

■

Can they be serious?

Are the Rev. Al Sharpton and Roy Innis, head of the Congress of
Racial Equality, really intent upon donning boxing gloves and taking to
the ring to settle their bitter feud?

The two New York activists have agreed to a public bout — to bene-
fit charity — as an encore to the sparring they engaged in on the set of
The Morton Downey, Jr. Show a few weeks ago.

Sharpton, who has drawn national media attention as the spokesper-
son for Tawana Brawley — the black teen-ager whose claim of rape at
the hands of six white men has been rejected by a New York grand jury
— was pushed to the floor by Innis during a taping of Downey's TV
show. The two men have argued over Brawley's claim and Sharpton's
role in the case. Both are notorious bad guys of the New York activist
community.

Here's an idea. Why not guarantee the "winner" a fight with Mike
Tyson?

'Great White Hope'

WASHINGTON, April 26, 1989

I wonder as I wander. Footnotes on life from a black perspective.

Is Chicago Mayor Richard M. Daley the "Great White Hope" of that
racially splintered city or will he actually work to bring people together
as he has promised?

Daley, whose father reigned over Chicago politics for nearly 21 years,
was sworn in Monday to serve out the remainder of Harold Washington's term. Washington, the city's first black mayor, died in office last
year.

Given Chicago's history of racial politics, Daley's good intentions may not be enough to heal the rift between whites and African-Americans in the Windy City.

■

Talk about healing rifts. How long do you think it will take the Rev. Jesse Jackson and Ron Brown, the Democratic Party chairman, to bury the hatchet?

Jackson, whose home base is Chicago, is said to be absolutely livid over the support Brown gave Daley in his general election victory over black mayoral candidate Timothy Evans. Evans, a Democrat, ran in the general election as an independent.

Not too long ago, Brown and the former presidential candidate were allies. Brown managed Jackson's political activities during last year's Democratic National Convention.

Now, Jackson is telling friends that Brown, who is the DNC's first black chairman, went overboard in his support of Daley.

■

How long is the list of challengers to Washington Mayor Marion Barry likely to get?

While only one person — former DNC Treasurer Sharon Pratt Dixon — officially has entered the mayoral race, others appear to be massing at the starting line.

The day after Dixon announced her candidacy, Washington Police Chief Maurice Turner resigned amid reports that he is considering a campaign to unseat Barry in next year's Democratic primary. Add to this the word from Jackson backers that *Washington Post* Executive Editor Benjamin Bradlee is behind an effort to get the black Baptist minister to enter the city's mayoral sweepstakes.

Jackson, who also maintains a residence in Washington, is said to be considering throwing his hat into the ring only if Barry decides not to seek re-election.

■

Are blacks really better athletes?

That's the question Tom Brokaw set out to answer Tuesday with an hour-long television show that makes me wonder how such a program ever made it to the air. One possible reason: The network doesn't have any African-Americans in senior news management jobs.

It may come as a surprise to NBC executives, but not to me, that blacks excel in track, basketball and football. Visit any ghetto in the United States and you will quickly understand why. You won't find many swimming pools, tennis courts or ice-skating rinks.

Do white Canadians dominate professional ice hockey because they are physically superior to the rest of us, or because they grow up in the icy reaches of the American hemisphere where, for most youngsters, ice hockey is the playground equivalent of basketball?

■

How does this bit of news make you feel?

Police in Cambridge, Md., finally cracked down on Darcy Bradley, a local character known for tooling about town in a drunken state.

Bradley, who has a history of public drunkenness, was stopped three times in one 24-hour period earlier this month and charged with drunken driving. Each time, the arresting officers released Bradley into the custody of his daughter after getting him to promise not to drive again while intoxicated.

At the time, local police explained that it was their policy to send drunken drivers home instead of to jail because of the need to hold jail space for more serious offenders.

But when 11 days later Bradley again was caught driving in a drunken stupor, local police put their foot down and carted him off to jail.

Now doesn't that just make you MADD?

■

Talk about things that make me mad. Who has time to sympathize over the social circumstances of the eight New York teen-agers charged with the brutal rape and beating that left their victim in a coma?

A few in New York's black community have blamed the attack on poverty and the discriminatory environment in which the young boys, ages 13 to 17, live. But many other residents of the attackers' Harlem neighborhood have generated an impressive outpouring of concern for the white victim. Some of them held a prayer vigil outside the hospital where the victim clings to life.

There'll be more than enough time to examine such social phenomena after those guilty of this ugly crime have been tried, convicted and given lengthy prison terms.

Like minds

WASHINGTON, Feb. 11, 1986

I wonder as I wander. Footnotes on life from a black perspective.

Did Ronald Reagan knowingly quote Franklin Roosevelt out of context during his recent State of the Union address when he implied that he and the former Democratic president were of like minds on the issue of welfare reform?

Reagan said, "As Franklin Roosevelt warned 51 years ago before this chamber: Welfare is a 'narcotic, a subtle destroyer of the human spirit.' "

But what Reagan failed to recount was that Roosevelt went on to offer these solutions to the problem of welfare reform:

1. Continue public aid to unemployable welfare recipients, or,

2. Create a federally funded jobs program to put the remainder back to work.

Given Reagan's reluctance to embrace these liberal notions, his speech writers understandably cut short the Roosevelt quote — giving new meaning to the saying, "out of sight, out of mind."

■

Have you noticed that another American tradition is biting the dust?

It seems that bootblacks are fast becoming more white than black. That's right. In hotels and malls across the country, the number of non-black bootblacks is on the rise. In Dallas and Tampa, for example, you can find white women, dressed in Tuxedo pants and shirts, shining shoes. In one Washington suburb, the bootblack in a fashionable mall is an Asian.

Now, I know why it is that black unemployment is still twice that of whites, at a time when the Reagan administration claims to have created millions of new jobs — blame it on the decline of the "black" bootblack. It seems they have gone the way of black jockeys.

■

Here's a quiz for you. What do blacks think of Ronald Reagan?

A. Forty-six percent think he is doing a good job.

B. Twenty-seven percent think he is doing a good job.

C. Fifty-six percent like the job he is doing.

D. Fifty-six percent believe he's a racist.

E. All of the above.

The answer is "E" — that is if you believe what you read recently in the Gallup Poll, the Lou Harris Survey, *The New York Times* Poll and a poll commissioned by *The Washington Post*.

What we need now is a poll to determine what blacks think of pollsters.

■

What is the significance of this?

Simon Wiesenthal, the much-heralded Nazi hunter, has taken on new prey. He is in search of opinions — of black Americans.

Yes, that's right. The man who helped bring Adolph Eichmann to justice has commissioned a national survey of the attitudes of blacks "toward the state of Israel and about Jews in general."

The results, published in December, focused largely on Louis Farrakhan and Jesse Jackson. Talk about an obsession.

■

Here's one for the "I think I overreacted" column.

When the president of the National Press Club found out that security personnel guarding Louis Farrakhan violated her directive and frisked reporters attending his press conference there, she barred the controversial Black Muslim minister from making future use of the press club.

You would think that such a harsh action wouldn't be necessary. If reporters don't want to submit to such searches, they should not attend Farrakhan press conferences — a blasphemous suggestion in this "pack journalism" town. The reality is that wherever Farrakhan holds his press conferences in Washington, reporters will attend and submit to his security checks.

Which just goes to prove that even journalists give in to occasional obsessions.

■

Talk about redundant.

The 1986 version of the National Urban League's State of Black America report is out, and it reads like a rewrite of every previous report, dating back to 1977. It makes you wonder whether anybody ever reads these things.

If the 220-page report is too lengthy for your reading habits, here is a synopsis: "Things are bad and getting worse."

Fire at will

Isn't it ironic that every year since 1977, American presidents have told us in their State of the Union messages that things are good and getting better?

■

Have you given any thought to why so many black men are up in arms over the movie *The Color Purple?*

Well, I didn't understand either until I watched the CBS broadcast of Bill Moyers' special, *The Vanishing Family — Crisis in Black America.* Combined, the two make black men look like a cross between Attila the Hun and Roman Polanski.

It will take a millennium (or at least six more prime-time programs like *The Cosby Show)* to undo the perceptual damage.

THE AUTHOR

**e**WAYNE Wickham began his journalism career in 1973 as a copyediting intern with the *Richmond Times Dispatch*. He has worked as a reporter for both the *Evening Sun* and *Sun* of Baltimore; and as a Capitol Hill correspondent for *U.S. News & World Report*. He also served as Washington correspondent and contributing editor for *Black Enterprise* magazine.

Wickham also has worked as a broadcast journalist, hosting a weekly public affairs program on WBAL-TV in Baltimore since 1983.

He holds a B.S. degree in journalism from the University of Maryland and a master's of public administration degree from the University of Baltimore. Wickham also earned a certificate in Afro-American Studies from the University of Maryland.

A founding member of the National Association of Black Journalists, he served as the organization's president from August 1987 to August 1989.

He joined Gannett News Service as a columnist in August 1985. ■

OTHER TITLES

USA TODAY Books is the imprint for books by Gannett New Media, a division of Gannett Co. Inc., with headquarters at 1000 Wilson Blvd., Arlington, Va. 22209.

For more information or to order this or other USA TODAY books, write to USA TODAY Books, P.O. Box 450, Washington, D.C. 20044, or phone 800-654-6931. In Virginia, phone 703-276-5942.

And Still We Rise:
Interviews with 50 Black Role Models

Barbara Reynolds
Epilogue by Coretta Scott King
Pages: 224. Paperback.

A celebration of success and accomplishment in the USA. Features conversations with 50 men and women who share their insights and offer examples for success. Retail price: $7.95, shipping extra. ISBN: 0-944347-02-9. Publisher: USA TODAY Books.

World Power Up Close

Allen H. Neuharth
With Jack Kelley and Laura E. Chatfield
Pages: 224. Hardbound.

This is the story of world power — told by 31 leaders who hold it: Presidents. Prime ministers. And other key leaders. The up close and personal story of their power, prestige and politics. Included: Behind-the-scenes anecdotes and impressions of each leader; revealing, detailed profiles; overviews of each country; close-up photos; the leaders' thoughts — in their own words. Retail price: $12.95, shipping extra. ISBN: 0-944347-19-3. Publisher: USA TODAY Books.

Nearly One World

Allen H. Neuharth
With Jack Kelley and Juan J. Walte
Pages: 257. Hardbound.

From Michael Jackson and Mikhail Gorbachev to our flourishing faith and women's rights, the world's cultural, economic and political barriers are falling. Global communications, universal trends and common aspirations are making the world's people more alike than they are different. Based on a 148,261-mile newsgathering assignment to 32 countries. Retail price: $18.95, shipping extra. ISBN: 0-385-26387-2. Publisher: Doubleday (New York, N.Y.).

Window on the World
Faces, Places and Plain Talk from 32 Countries

Allen H. Neuharth
Pages: 240. Hardbound.

USA TODAY JetCapade's 32-country world tour visits princes and presidents, beggars and boatmen, capitalists and communists. Includes more than 500 full-color photographs, interviews with world leaders, full-color flags and maps. Retail price: $24.95, shipping extra. ISBN: 0-944347-16-9. Publisher: USA TODAY Books.

Truly One Nation

Allen H. Neuharth
With Ken Paulson and Dan Greaney
Pages: 144. Hardbound.

A journalistic journey that took a team of reporters to all 50 states in six months. It found a nation of diverse people, philosophies, politics. But above all, a nation united. Examines everyday life in the USA, from religion to recreation, politics to patriotism, civil rights to charity. Retail price: $19.95, shipping extra. ISBN: 0-385-26180-2. Publisher: Doubleday (New York, N.Y.).

Plain Talk Across the USA

Allen H. Neuharth
Pages: 320. Hardbound.

Full color throughout with more than 500 photographs and interviews with people in all 50 states. Features details on all 50 states and conversations with notable personalities from each state. Retail price: $16.95, shipping extra. ISBN: 0-944347-00-2. Publisher: USA TODAY Books.

Profiles of Power:
How the Governors Run Our 50 States

Allen H. Neuharth
With Ken Paulson and Phil Pruitt
Pages: 256. Hardbound.

Today's governors are no longer back-slapping "good ol' boys." Today's governors — men and women — are modern managers. With profiles of and interviews with each governor. Retail price: $9.95, shipping extra. ISBN: 0-944347-14-2. Publisher: USA TODAY Books.

OTHER TITLES

USA Citizens Abroad: A Handbook

American Citizens Abroad
Pages: 128. Paperback.

A usable guide to living or traveling outside the USA, written by U.S. citizens living overseas. Tips on taxes, voting, going to school, personal finance, customs and how to get help. Retail price: $9.95, shipping extra. ISBN: 0-944347-13-4. Publisher: USA TODAY Books.

The Making of McPaper:
The Inside Story of USA TODAY

Peter Prichard
Pages: 384. Hardbound.

When USA TODAY was launched on Sept. 15, 1982, many journalists laughed at it and called it "McPaper," the titan of "junk food journalism." Now it is called No. 1, the USA's most widely read newspaper. A candid look at the ups and downs along the way. Retail price: $19.95, shipping extra. ISBN: 0-8362-7939-5. Publisher: Andrews & McMeel (Kansas City, Mo.).

Also available in paperback: Pages: 416. Retail price: $5.95, shipping extra. ISBN: 0-312-91168-8. Publisher: St. Martin's Press (New York, N.Y.).

The USA TODAY Cartoon Book

Charles Barsotti, Bruce Cochran, Dean Vietor
Paperback

Cartoons from the pages of USA TODAY's Life, Sports and Money sections. Funny, but filled with insight into our lives, our work and our play. Retail price: $6.95, shipping extra. ISBN: 0-8362-2077-3. Publisher: Andrews & McMeel (Kansas City, Mo.).

Portraits of the USA

Edited by Acey Harper and Richard Curtis
Pages: 144. Hardbound.

Glossy, high-quality coffee-table book. Features photos taken for USA TODAY, many of which are award winners. Photos are portraits of life in the USA, seen through the eyes of USA TODAY's photographers and selected by USA TODAY editors. Retail price: $37.95, shipping extra. ISBN: 87491-815-4. Publisher: Acropolis Books Ltd. (Washington, D.C.).

OTHER TITLES

USA TODAY Crossword Puzzle Book
Volumes I, II, III, IV and V

Charles Preston
Paperback

A series of puzzles from USA TODAY's crossword puzzle editor. Each volume contains 60 puzzles never before published in book form. Retail price: $5.95 each, shipping extra. Publisher: Putnam (New York, N.Y.).